ABOUT ISLAND PRESS

Since 1984, the nonprofit organization Island Press has been stimulating, shaping, and communicating ideas that are essential for solving environmental problems worldwide. With more than 800 titles in print and some 40 new releases each year, we are the nation's leading publisher on environmental issues. We identify innovative thinkers and emerging trends in the environmental field. We work with world-renowned experts and authors to develop cross-disciplinary solutions to environmental challenges.

Island Press designs and executes educational campaigns in conjunction with our authors to communicate their critical messages in print, in person, and online using the latest technologies, innovative programs, and the media. Our goal is to reach targeted audiences—scientists, policymakers, environmental advocates, urban planners, the media, and concerned citizens—with information that can be used to create the framework for long-term ecological health and human well-being.

Island Press gratefully acknowledges major support of our work by The Agua Fund, The Andrew W. Mellon Foundation, Betsy & Jesse Fink Foundation, The Bobolink Foundation, The Curtis and Edith Munson Foundation, Forrest C. and Frances H. Lattner Foundation, G.O. Forward Fund of the Saint Paul Foundation, Gordon and Betty Moore Foundation, The Kresge Foundation, The Margaret A. Cargill Foundation, The Overbrook Foundation, The S.D. Bechtel, Jr. Foundation, The Summit Charitable Foundation, Inc., V. Kann Rasmussen Foundation, The Wallace Alexander Gerbode Foundation, and other generous supporters.

The opinions expressed in this book are those of the author(s) and do not necessarily reflect the views of our supporters.

THE NATURE OF URBAN DESIGN

THE NATURE OF

URBAN DESIGN

A New York Perspective on Resilience

ALEXANDROS WASHBURN

Washington | Covelo | London

Library of Congress Cataloging-in-Publication Data
Washburn, Alexandros.
  The nature of urban design : a New York perspective on resilience / by Alexandros Washburn.
    pages cm
  Includes bibliographical references and index.
  ISBN 978-1-61091-380-5 (cloth : alk. paper) -- ISBN 1-61091-380-9 (cloth : alk. paper) 1. City planning--New York (State)--New York. I. Title.
  HT168.N5W37 2013
  307.1'21609747--dc23
                    2013014789

Manufactured in the United States of America
10 9 8 7 6 5 4 3 2 1

Island Press would like to thank Furthermore: a program of the J. M. Kaplan Fund for generous support of the design and printing of this book.

page i: Prague's resilient waterfront.
(Credit: Alexandros Washburn)

page iii: Athena in the south cove of Battery Park City, a few blocks from Wall Street.
(Credit: Alexandros Washburn)

Book design by Roberto & Fearn de Vicq de Cumptich

Keywords: civic virtue; climate change adaptation; climate change mitigation; density bonus; greenhouse gas emissions; the High Line, PlaNYC; planned retreat; Red Hook, Brooklyn; sustainability; transit-oriented development; urban resilience; zoning regulation

Printed on recycled, acid-free paper

Dedicated to Daniel Patrick Moynihan

Hurricane Irene moves in.
(Credit: Alexandros Washburn)

CONTENTS

wrote this book out of a sense of self-preservation. I had to convince some very powerful people to do what they otherwise wouldn't do. I had just become the chief urban designer for New York City at the Department of City Planning and entered with the notion that good design changed things. I immediately found out that I was naïve. No one was going to listen to me proffering sketchy notions of good design.

They wanted to build bigger buildings. The mega-developers, power-lawyers, and "starchitects" that fuel the riot of construction that makes New York new every day wanted to do things their way. And as I got to know the full spectrum of stakeholders, I saw that it was not just the rich, the powerful, or the famous that sought to change things. The stakeholders were also the community leaders and the homeowners and the small-business owners, and they also had ideas about what they wanted and what they didn't want. Everybody I met with every day had a loud interest in what the city was becoming. There was energy, but not consensus.

To survive I had to communicate a common design interest, and for that I needed more than sketches. I needed a political, a financial, and a design framework to relate the full spectrum of individual actors with a common good. The mayor's announcement of PlaNYC in 2007 gave me the basis of that framework. The purpose of the plan was to make the city sustainable. I took the premise that urban design could make the city sustainable. With a grant from the Rockefeller Foundation, I set out to turn a bubble diagram into an explanation of how we were going to change the city through the nature of urban design. I began to devote my nights to writing in order to string together what I knew instinctively was the right thing to do, but I had to be able to make a cogent case for it during the day. I had to persuade people that the common good of PlaNYC would make the individual actions they sought—the individual buildings they sought to build—better for their neighborhood, more profitable for their developers, and more resilient for their city. What were the purpose, the process, and the products of urban design? How was urban design going to satisfy their objectives while at the same time change New York City for the better?

I could not have begun to explain the nature and complexity of urban design without having had the benefit of a mentor, someone who had spent a lifetime fighting to improve cities, who had managed to integrate politics, finance, and design into the fabric of his own career. My mentor was Daniel Patrick Moynihan, for whom I served as public works advisor in the 1990s. Moynihan was the only senator on Capitol Hill who thought it worth having an architect on staff.

He had died shortly after retiring from the U.S. Senate, after the election of his successor, Hillary Rodham Clinton. He had been hoping for a long twilight of writing books in the old schoolhouse next to his country home in upstate New York with his beautiful wife, Liz, and a growing set of grandchildren. But it wasn't to be, and in 2003, I was wandering the halls of the Maxwell School of Citizenship and Public Affairs at Syracuse University, his alma mater, looking for his memorial service.

The service would be packed with others who considered him their mentor as well; his former staff were about in the world as members of Congress, cabinet secretaries, ambassadors, judges, authors, professors,

even television stars. He had been a magnet for intellect in a broad range of fields. The political scientist Michael Barone had called him "the nation's best thinker among politicians since Lincoln, and its best politician among thinkers since Jefferson." What had attracted me to him was his record of building. He was the one who had transformed Pennsylvania Avenue in Washington, D.C., from a slum to America's Main Street, who had fought to reverse the effects of highways on America's downtowns, and who had saved numerous landmarks of architecture from destruction, including Louis Sullivan's first skyscraper in Buffalo and Grand Central Terminal in New York City.

I had come to him late in his political life, and I had no ambitions in politics. In 1993, I was a young architect dissatisfied that architecture seemed incapable of improving the city I had grown up in, Washington, D.C., which was descending into the anarchy of a crack epidemic. No matter how many architecture awards the buildings designed by the firm I worked for won, the city kept getting worse and worse. I thought maybe government could help, and I was told there was one powerful person in government who cared about architecture—Daniel Patrick Moynihan.

I got an unpaid internship in a back room writing memos. Apparently he liked my writing, and one day he asked, "Who is this Washburn fellow?" His chief of staff told him I was an architect working in the back. "An architect? Bring him in!" He met me, he liked me, and he hired me as his public works advisor. I began what felt like the most incredible seminar in design I could possibly have imagined. Moynihan did indeed like the subject of architecture, and while the other staff would wait in line to present their memos on health care, I would get a call to meet the senator for lunch to discuss mine.

I soon began to realize that it wasn't architecture itself that he was interested in. It was architecture as a tool of building cities; in effect, as a tool of building citizens. His relationship to architecture was personal. You wouldn't know it from his impeccable dress and manor, but he grew up desperately poor in a broken home in Hell's Kitchen in New York City. His mother tended bar after his father left. His education was not a matter of priority. Indeed, what education he had came from the streets of New York. But the lesson he learned from the streets was not about being a neighborhood tough. It was about being a citizen. When he was a teenager, he was skinny and smart and tended to run his Irish mouth, which got him in trouble frequently with the neighborhood bullies.

He would tell me stories of how he would shine shoes for quarters on the steps of the New York Public Library, underneath the watchful gaze of the twin stone lions. And that, he said, is where he learned about life. He was street smart, certainly, like his fellow urchins. But he said he learned something from the public spaces where he put down his shoe-shine kit, and from the conversations he had with his customers. It didn't matter that he was poor and the shoes he polished might be a millionaire's. Everyone was equal in the public space. His intellect was treated with respect. It didn't matter that he lived in a small apartment above where his mother tended bar; his outdoor teenage life was lived in the glorious civic spaces of the metropolis. Those public spaces taught him to respect and be respected and gave him entry to a broader world than he would go home to.

As he entered public life first as an aide to Governor Harriman and then to President Kennedy, he told me of the meetings and power brokering that got things built. He was in the room when Robert Moses, New York City's "master builder," would enter unsmiling into a meeting with the governor. Moses would hand him an envelope with the list of projects he wanted approved written in pencil on the cover, and then he would leave. No discussion. Just power from the ultimate power broker. That was the extent of planning in New York of the 1950s.

In addition to the larger than life stories, he also told me of the ridiculous situations that can color the success of public works. For instance, he spoke about how he went to pick up the architect of the new Pennsylvania Avenue from his hotel room so he could testify before Congress about the plans and secure governmental approval that would revolutionize public space. He found the architect in his underwear so drunk and obstreperous that the only way he could think to avert the disaster of him presenting in such a state was to hide his pants and leave.

I thought of myself as pretty fortunate to be hearing firsthand all these strategies, tactics, and foibles of city building. I didn't stop to think why—if I were the public works advisor to the senator, why was I the one getting all the advice from the senator?

About a year into my tenure there, the senator brought up a project that was important to him. He wanted to rebuild Pennsylvania Station. Penn Station had been considered America's greatest train station and the finest piece of public architecture in New York City. It had stood near the Hell's Kitchen neighborhood of his childhood, and Moynihan remembered its vast halls, and the daily dance of crowds under its Roman arches. It was torn down in 1963 and dumped into the New Jersey marshes in order to sell off its air rights to a sports arena and office building. The neighborhood had never quite recovered, and Moynihan wanted to set it right.

Moynihan insisted we form a corporation and went about the business of approvals and funding. It was a herculean task, but he was at the pinnacle of power. Governors and presidents pitched in to help. He decided that I should move to New York to get it up and running. We had lunch the last day I worked for him. As we left, he turned to me and said, "Alex, make it inevitable."

And with that, I threw myself into the task; I took on a hydra-headed monster of politics, money, and design to get it done. I succeeded in some aspects, failed in others. But yes, I made it inevitable.

He did not know that yet when he died. He would never see the improvements that he fought for. It pained me as I walked down the hall at the Maxwell School. What good was all his time with me, all this teaching, all this effort if he couldn't live to see his train station built? I cursed myself. Couldn't I have worked faster? Couldn't I have cut some corners?

I heard some voices approaching; the memorial would be starting soon. I lifted my head from my dejection. And then I saw the inscription on the wall that Moynihan would have passed every day. It was the Oath of the Athenians that young men took on reaching adulthood in the ancient city. It was a pledge to uphold the laws and revere the gods, and to leave their city better than they found it.

I saw now why, during our lunches, when I had managed to say something worthwhile, Moynihan's highest praise was to tell me, "spoken like a true Athenian."

I then realized that my years with Moynihan were not about architecture; they were about civic virtue. Civic virtue is about doing something that will not benefit you—it will benefit a future generation. Civic virtue is about leaving the city better than you found it. Moynihan spent all that time and effort with me to transmit to me a set of values, which I only later discovered that I bore the responsibility of transmitting to others. When he said, "make it inevitable," he wasn't just talking about the train station. He was talking about transmitting a definition of civic virtue to the next generation. He was telling me to leave the city better than I found it, and to teach the next generation of urban designers their responsibility and their opportunity.

— April 5, 2013

had no idea that writing books is harder than building cities. The enormous sense of relief I feel at *having written* fills me with the joyous desire to say THANK YOU to all those who have helped me. And as hard as it may be to write a book, putting up with its author during the writing is harder still. So THANK YOU as well to those who have tolerated me in the process.

First thanks for both help and tolerance go to the **Rockefeller Foundation.** Without their support and infinite patience (it's been over five years), the ideas now in this book would have remained little more than scribbles and diagrams in my notebooks. **Judith Rodin, Darren Walker** (now with the Ford Foundation), **Joan Shigekawa** (now with the National Endowment for the Arts), **Eddie Torres,** and **Don Roeseke,** thank you. I hope that this book can fulfill your tradition of quality in both thought and action and achieve the real-world results you have set as a standard in your philanthropy.

Next I want to thank all those at the **New York City Department of City Planning** whose insight, caring, collegiality, and infinite curiosity about the city helped me shape the ideas that shaped this book. First, my incomparable associates in the Urban Design Division. **Jeff Shumaker, Skye Duncan, Thaddeus Pawlowski,** and **Erick Gregory** are brilliant as well as compassionate. I say this because unlike other arts, where technical skill matters most, urban design demands empathy. It is difficult to be a good urban designer without being a good person, and **Jeff, Skye, Thad,** and **Erick** are very, very good. I could not be prouder that we have shared a unique moment in shaping New York together.

The urban design division acts as the design eyes of the department, and it is from my colleagues there, three hundred strong, that we learned to see this city as it might become. The intellectual curiosity of the department is an invaluable aid to the growth of the city, and my thanks go to **every single employee of the New York City Department of City Planning.** Space doesn't allow naming them all, but I have to give particular thanks to the **Policy Committee,** and to **David Karnovsky,** our chief counsel, **Richard Barth,** our executive director, and the constellation of wonderful colleagues such as **Cecilia Kushner, Eric Kober, Sandy Hornick, Patrick Too, Frank Ruchala, Sarah Goldwyn, Justin Moore, Julie Lubin, Barry Dinerstein,** and **Irene Sadko,** along with Jean Davis and Bruni Mesa, just to name a few. Then there is **Tom Wargo, Beth Lieberman, Chris Holme, Claudia Herasme** and the brilliant literate ranks of the zoning division, our neighbors and alter egos of urban design. Thanks as well to our borough directors: **Edith Hsu Chen, Purnima Kapur, Carol Samol,** **Len Garcia,** and **John Young.** I also want to thank the unceasing army of summer volunteers who have come to draw with us in the urban design division from all over the world. No continent save Antarctica is unrepresented. These young people come to learn from us, but it always turns out we learn more from them. They bring their perspective on urban design from every corner of the globe, and make New York a richer city.

And of course, the greatest thanks go to **Amanda Burden,** chair of the City Planning Commission and director of the Department of City Planning. She brought urban design back as a division and a priority. She is a never-ceasing advocate for the quality of public space, and her belief in the value of urban design has made it a force in shaping the city. Thank you, Amanda!

There are many in the Bloomberg administration beyond City Planning whom I would also like to thank. Those without long experience in government don't realize the unique decade we have lived through. It is rare that government can accomplish so much change in a city, rarer still that it can attract officials and staff who can daily work across the full spectrum of agencies as a team, indeed, even as friends. First there is the mayor, himself. Thank you, **Mayor Mike,** for insisting on quality in the public realm, and tolerating the scruffy man with no tie who was your urban designer. I thank Deputy Mayors **Dan Doctoroff, Patti Harris, Robert Steel, Kevin Sheekey;** Commissioners **Janette Sadik-Khan;** (she is amazing through and through) at the Department of Transportation, **Adrian Benepe** at Parks, **Shaun Donovan** (now Secretary Donovan) and **Matt Wambua** at the Department of Housing Preservation and Development, **Bob LiMandri** at the Department of Buildings, and **Marc Jahr** at the Housing Development Corporation, as well as **Cas Holloway,** now deputy mayor, then commissioner at the Department of

Environmental Protection. I want to give particular thanks to **Rohit Aggarwala,** who founded the Office of Long-Term Planning and Sustainability, with whose staff we worked so closely to build an image of a sustainable city. And of course, the city has so many stars in every department, such as **James Colgate, Adam Freed, Margaret Newman, Andy Wiley Schwartz,** and **Wendy Feuer**. We made hay while the sun shone.

This book is dedicated to Senator Moynihan, and in the foreword you find out why. But a dedication to Pat Moynihan is also a dedication to the many others touched by him in a long life of mentoring. Those include people as diverse as **Richard Sennett** and **K**evin Sheekey, Judge Eaton** with his stellar wife, **Susan Henshaw Jones,** and a list too numerous to thank individually, but to whom I owe deep thanks. Especially so to Pat's wife, **Liz Moynihan,** and daughter **Maura,** whose affection and support have been necessary to maintain a sense of purpose over the long term. As Pat used to tell me, "city building is not for the short winded."

I have been most fortunate to work with the best doers and thinkers in urban design in the city, and their successes and personal inspiration are fundamental to the optimism of this book. First, thanks to my friends at the High Line, to **Joshua David, Robert Hammond,** and **Peter Mullan.** Thanks to **John Alschuler** and to **Jerold Kayden,** who know the value of public space better than any others. Thanks to **Barry Bergdoll** at the Museum of Modern **Art** and **Anne Guiney** at the Institute for Urban Design. Professor **Nikos Salingaros** of Berkeley gave me new insight into the mathematics of urban design and did so with great friendship and humility.

I have special thanks to those designers and friends who had to submit their works to me for criticism at City Planning. Most, I hope, remain friends. In the process of working together, I of course learned far more from you than you may have learned from me. Thanks then to **Bjarke Ingels,** to **Christian de Portzamparc, Gregg Pasquarelli, Liz Diller,** and **Ric Scofidio; James Corner, Enrique Norten, Steven Holl, Toshiko Mori, Jamie Carpenter, Lee Weintraub, Claire Weisz, Michael Van Valkenburgh, Matt Urbanski; Gene Kohn, Jill Lerner, Bill Pederson,** and **Paul Katz; David Childs** and **Rafael Pelli; Bob Fox** and **Rick Cook; Marion Weiss** and **Michael Manfredi; Linda Pollak** and **Sandro Marpillero; Stan Eckstut** and **Rick Parisi.** And of course, **Ann Looper** at the American Institute of Landscape Architects and **Rick Bell** at the American Institute of Architects. This is not a complete list, and my thanks go to all.

If I learned from my colleagues on projects here in New York, I learned another perspective from my colleagues around the world. I can not thank my international urban designer friends enough, whether I was meeting with you at our studio, strolling down the High Line with you, or seeing projects with you in your home country. All of you informed my thinking about New York and the place of cities in the world. Thank you to **Lang Ng, Lay Bee Yap, Ng Lye Hock, Fun Siew Leng,** and **Goh Chok Tong** of Singapore; **K. K. Ling** and **Sujata Govada** in Hong Kong; **Jurgen Bruns-Berentelg** in Germany; **Mayor Xu Qin** and **Wang Peng** of Shenzen; **Ricardo Pereira Leite, Miguel Bucalem, Elizabete Franca,** and **Maria Teresa Deniz** from Brazil; **Larry Parsons, Sophie Patitsas, Rob Adams,** and **Marcus Westbury** in Australia; **Kaila Colbin** in New Zealand; **Thomas Hudecek** and **Martin Barry** in Prague; and my many dear friends in Holland, including **Henk Ovink, George Brugmans,** and **Ruud Reutelingsperger.** The urban design world is always growing.

Which brings me to offer sincere thanks to a unique thought leader in the world of urban design, Professor **Ricky Burdett** of the London School of Economics and New York University, founder of Urban Age. Ricky and his fellow directors at Urban Age have a peerless understanding of cities, and his support and camaraderie has been vital.

I want to offer great thanks to **Eric Sanderson,** a good friend whose explorations of human habitats in Mannahatta have opened our eyes to the sustainable possibilities latent in cities. He doesn't just understand biology as a science, he understands people. Working with him is to understand the power of gentleness. Thank you, Eric!

I want to thank **Vishaan Chakrabarti,** who thought of me for my current role, and who has worked with me at every scale with good humor and his own brand of brilliance. (Washburns and Chakrabartis were surprised to discover they are distant cousins by marriage from a past century and adjacent mountain villages in Greece; if that's not an example of globalization, I don't know what is.)

In the production of this book, I would like to thank my first editorial team from Metropolis, **Suzan Szenasy** and **Martin Pedersen** and **Diana Murphy.** Their kindness and passion for design launched the book. I also want to thank **Lisa Chamberlain,** who helped not just as a family member but as an editor in the first manuscript. Her perspective and very fine style of writing helped the book to grow. And I want to thank **Isobel Herbold** and **Mack Cole-Edelsack,** who assisted with visuals and manuscript. **David Bragdon, Alex Marshall, Carolo Steinman,** and **Jeff Speck** offered wonderful perspective as readers.

But the hardest task in the very hard task of writing is to finish the book. I am completely indebted to **Heather Boyer** and my team at Island Press for helping me reach that goal and do so in a way far better than I could have done myself. Thank you to Heather, and to **Rebecca Bright, Sharis Simonian, Jaime Jennings, Courtney Lix, Maureen Gately, David Miller,** and **Chuck Savitt.** Heather is a prolific and focused editor. Because she cares so much about cities and knows so much about resilience, the book matured under her direction. She focused, she read and re-read, she brought out the essentials. She directed with tact and firmness, and it is her editing that brought this book to completion. And I cannot express my thanks enough to the superbly talented designers of this book, **Fearn** and **Roberto de Vicq de Cumptich,** who understand the soul of cities and make every review a surprise and delight.

In closing, I want to thank **Barbara Wilks,** my partner at W Architecture and Landscape Architecture, LLC, with whom I learned, thought, and practiced in the relation of nature to the city. She was a caring supporter both personally and professionally. At Penn, she was the last student of Ian McHarg and the first student of James Corner, and her life and work have brought nature and architecture together. Her designs and built works have a confident beauty.

The greatest thanks of all go to the rest of my family, who both helped and tolerated me, with no gain and only sacrifice to themselves. My daughters **Sophia, Athena, Lelia,** and **Simone;** the mothers of my children, **Monica** and **Lisa;** my mother and father, **Lelia Kanavarioti** and **Wilcomb Washburn,** both authors, both professors, now deceased. I hope at least they are proud. No one in my family has not been affected by the demands of this book. I give you both my thanks and, yes, my apologies.

And many thanks to my wife, **Samar Maziad,** for her faith and affection.

Flooding in the wake of Hurricane Sandy in Red Hook, Brooklyn. (Credit: Erick Gregory)

The last time the mayor ordered an evacuation of my neighborhood in Brooklyn was for Hurricane Irene. That was last year, and I obediently packed up and stayed with family on high ground in Manhattan while the storm passed. Now the evacuation order is for Hurricane Sandy. But this time, I am not leaving. I know it's somewhat irresponsible to stay, especially because I work for the mayor who ordered the evacuation. Because I'm the chief urban designer for New York City, I want to observe the effects of the storm and particularly the dynamics of the storm surge on streets and structures. I know enough professionally about the dangers that a storm the size of Sandy poses to the city that I should be worried.

All the coastal neighborhoods in New York City are ordered evacuated—the Far Rockaways as well as Wall Street. As long as you are coastal, in zone A, you are supposed to leave. That's more than 350,000 people. My neighborhood is Red Hook, in Brooklyn, about a mile from downtown Manhattan where the East River meets upper New York Harbor. They used to make ships in Red Hook, and you could say ships used to make Red Hook, too. Much of the neighborhood is built on cobblestone fill brought over as ballast in the nineteenth century. The neighborhood was covered in factories and warehouses, all brick, now occupied by artisans and grocers. When not flooded, it is a beautiful neighborhood, with views of the skyscrapers of Lower Manhattan and the Statue of Liberty.

When I go outside to check the level of the storm surge, if a police patrol stops me, I plan to show him my city ID and say that I'm conducting research. The lights are flickering, the wind is really picking up, and as I write this, I know I should probably move away from the windows in case they shatter. The guy on the first floor evacuated a long time ago. I comfort myself with the thought that I'm on the second floor. Even if the storm surge is the full eleven feet, I'm at twelve feet. Right? It's the cocktail hour, and I am having my customary martini. No sense in curtailing my routine. High tide will be at 8 p.m., which unfortunately coincides with landfall for the hurricane, which unfortunately coincides with the full moon. So the storm surge is amplified by an extra high gravitational tide.

The subway shut down last night. We will lose power any minute now, which will force me to leave my computer and get out pencil and paper and use a candle if I want to continue writing. In the meantime,

I can check the Internet. A crane is in danger of collapsing in Manhattan, one thousand feet above Midtown. The first fatality is reported in Queens. And there's a blog post about Red Hook, about how the water is seeping up Van Brunt Street.

I look outside and see a trickle of water in the gutter. Nothing unusual, except that the water is flowing *out* of the gutter, and the trickle is turning rapidly into a stream. I put on my rubber boots and go downstairs. I open the door and water rushes in, dark water covered in the golden leaves of autumn. I step out into the street but realize that I'd better not—there's a current—and as my hallway fills, the basement too must be filling and that's where the electrical panel is. It shorts out. The lights flicker, I hear the breakers fall. Then there is an explosion outside, and the neighborhood goes dark.

Now it's all darkness, not black, but an eerie brown, and whatever light there is reflects off the water, which keeps on rising. My roof is leaking pretty badly now, but because I defied the evacuation order, I can put buckets under the leaks. A roof can stop a rain shower easily, but when rain is driven by high winds, it goes horizontal, and somehow it gets in.

I love New York, I love Red Hook, but I'm more than anxious now. The waters outside are rising farther and moving faster. I go upstairs to look out from the roof. The wind is too strong to go out on the roof; I'd risk being blown off. It's too dark to see what's going on in the backyard, but the street in front of me is now a full-fledged river. A neighbor left his car behind. I measure the flood by how much of the car I can see. The wheels go under, the doors, now just a

roofline. Debris is rushing by. Anyone not out or up on higher ground at this point has had it.

I am at the center of New York, surrounded by buildings, but those buildings are all separated by water. I try to think of Venice, but that's not what it feels like. The scene makes me think of buildings like boulders in a mountain river. Only a kayak would navigate these waters.

I have to trust that the surge will crest, and I use what little battery power is left in my computer to check the Internet and the path of the storm and the timing of the tides. I think we've reached the peak. I think my house will stand.

Tomorrow and the days following will be about recovery. Wet, cold recovery. Power won't be back for days. Much of the city will barely function.

I go to bed knowing only one thing—that tomorrow my neighbors will be out and talking together and helping each other. Each conversation will be a small stone resetting the foundation for our great community. We have so many families here, so many children. Creative people who could not afford the canyons of Manhattan found space here.

Is community enough, though, against forces so large? This storm is almost a thousand miles across. Maybe we are relying too much on the resilience of our citizens and not enough on the resilience of our city. I feel that the sense of community New York City inspires is strong, but I also feel that physically the city itself is weak, at least in the face of these storms. We have neglected these dangers to the city itself and left it vulnerable to these large forces. We tell ourselves that these are once-in-a-century storms, but two have come about in the space of a single year. Maybe they were once-in-a-century storms during the last century. This century, I think they will be far more frequent.

I go to bed knowing that if we care about cities, we have to do something. We have to change the status quo. I want my city to be safe.

WHY DO WE CARE ABOUT CITIES?

I care about my city because I care about my neighborhood. I care about my neighborhood because I care about my family. It is a natural progression, something I've watched in my children as they have grown in age and aptitude. The emancipation of leaving the house to walk to school ushered in the neighborhood, but when they learned to ride the subway and conquered the city itself, they became New Yorkers above all else.

I am sure the same can be said of Parisians and Paulistas, as it is true of the citizens of almost any city in the world. We care about our own cities.

Beyond emotion, there are economic, social, and cultural reasons we should all care about cities, and not just our own. For the first time in history, more than 50 percent of the world's population lives in cities, and the percentage is rising. The world depends on cities for jobs, for homes, for creative endeavor. Cities as a whole produce 80 percent of the world's wealth. They are the crucibles of culture, and advances in one city are transmitted and adopted in others with lightning speed. When cities improve, the world improves.

A study by McKinsey, the private-sector consultants, found that global production, and hence global wealth, is concentrated in the six hundred largest and fastest-growing cities in the world, whose composition is shifting decidedly toward cities in the south and east of the globe.[1]

There is a notion that cities grow haphazardly. There is a notion that cities are always changed by someone else. This book means to dispel these notions. Everything in a city is designed, and everyone in a city has a stake in the result.

It is the nature of urban design that we make cities in our own image, however consciously or unconsciously. We live with the results of what we make of our cities, paying for the mistakes with dystopia, enjoying the delight of getting it right.

Growth can exacerbate existing problems, or it can afford an opportunity to learn from our mistakes, adapt to new conditions, and make living in a city safer and more rewarding. Urban design is the art of changing cities, guiding growth to follow new patterns that better meet our challenges while improving our quality of life.

The world has long debated the quality of life in cities versus in the country. The divide between urban and rural is an ancient one. City mouse and country mouse. Throughout the ages, we have delighted in contrasting the culture of the two, from Aesop's fable to the Beverly Hillbillies. Behind the cultural images, of course, there are hard facts on the difference between urban and rural life. In China, a city dweller has more than triple the income of a rural dweller.[2] In India, urban women have almost double the rate of literacy of rural women.[3] Culturally, we highlight the virtues of rural life, but in reality the pull toward a better standard of living has been steadily toward cities. Apparently, to the consternation of Aesop's country mouse, we actually do prefer the city.

No more so than in the United States, which is the world's most urbanized large country. Eighty percent of U.S. citizens live in urbanized areas.[4] But if you asked these urbanized Americans if they lived in cities, more than half of them would say no. They would say they don't live in cities, they live in suburbs or small towns. And they would list the virtues that have been affixed to rural life as chief among their enjoyments. There is peace and quiet. There is space between houses, so much so that I know one man who moved to the suburbs because he "didn't want neighbors, he wanted to live on the frontier." True enough—in summertime when the trees were in leaf and the hedges full, he could not see his neighbors and could nourish his frontier fantasy. He even kept a rifle at the ready.

But this suburban man did have neighbors, and he had electrical power and a gas line, a sanitary sewer, and, of course, municipal water. Fiber optics, copper wire, cable, and a cell phone tower complete his communication package. And public employees pick up his trash and guard his house while he is sleeping, albeit with his squirrel gun under his bed. He drives every day to a job downtown and is not averse to shopping and dining in the harlot-sodden metropolis he otherwise goes to great pains to distance himself from. And perhaps the greatest indignity of all is that the U.S. Census Bureau takes no account of his wish to live on the frontier and instead counts his suburban home as urban: part of the metropolitan statistical area.

80% of U.S. citizens live in urbanized areas.

The point is, a suburb is a city. Economically, socially, infrastructurally, a suburb is simply a low-density city. And although I might caricature some of its adherents (as they might caricature latte-sipping metrosexual apartment dwellers downtown), the suburb is a beloved form of city for a very large portion of the population.

The suburb in opposition to the city is a substitute for the rural versus urban debate that was formative in America. Going back to Thomas Jefferson's vision of a nation of yeoman farmers versus Alexander Hamilton's notion of a nation of urbane bankers, city versus suburb is an emotional, moral, and political issue in the United States today as urban versus rural was in the nineteenth century. Except that everyone has already moved to cities. So in America today, suburb versus city has taken on the political and moral overtones that rural versus urban had in the early days of the republic.

Politics exaggerates the differences and skews decision making. A governor of New Jersey took money out of an urban transit project to link the Jersey suburbs with midtown Manhattan to score political points with his suburban base and redistribute the money to suburban road builders. The move resonated with suburban voters, even though in the long run, the lack of a tunnel will seriously hurt the metropolitan economy to which they are inextricably tied. Politics is local—very local—and successful politicians learn to exploit any difference. When you step back from the rhetoric, however, and stick to the metrics, you see that suburbs are cities, too.

CITIES ARE VULNERABLE

Perhaps it takes a disaster to cut through the politics and remind us that we are all in this together. The hurricane that hit New York City is the same hurricane that hit the Jersey suburbs. And now the governors of New Jersey and New York are talking about solidarity.

Ultimately, it is the recognition that cities (which by definition include suburbs) are vulnerable that can unite us. It has happened throughout history and is only natural. Because cities are where the wealth is, cities have always been vulnerable to invasion. Because cities are where the people are, cities have always been vulnerable to the rapid spread of disease. In the past, we have always been able to cope by taking citywide actions like building walls in fifth-century Constantinople against invaders or enacting sanitary and building codes in nineteenth-century New York against disease.

Now we are approaching a crisis of resilience in our cities. Sea levels are rising and storms are growing in intensity. What was once termed a "one hundred–year storm" now seems like an annual occurrence. Can cities, especially coastal cities, survive? I look out my window, and I see blocks of New York City still dark, three days after the storm passed. The *New York Times* reports it may be another ten days until power is restored. The lights on the Verrazano Bridge go on only halfway across its span, a mocking sign of our disruption.

THE ROLE OF URBAN DESIGN

If what cities need to do is adapt to a changing climate and mitigate their contribution to climate change, why are we talking about urban design? The future of the city lies in answering the question, "Is there a form of city that can survive the new extremes of weather, that can accommodate millions more citizens in dignity and prosperity, that can avoid contributing more to climate change, and still be worth living in?" Underlying the response is a belief that we can make the world sustainable if we make cities livable. Utopian, perhaps, but we don't have to wait to put our idealism to the test.

For an urban designer, making cities more resilient in the face of the common challenges (such as budget constraints) and the slightly less common (such as extreme weather events) must be achieved while improving civic life. Resilience itself is not civic life. A fortress of technology that could withstand tidal waves while emitting no carbon would not be an urban design success if it embittered its residents. I believe that to improve the quality of civic life, you begin by improving the quality of public space.

Knowing what we do about the form of cities and their relation to climate change, and knowing the transformative power of urban design to change their form to meet the challenges, people who care about cities are in a position to imagine a future city that will meet our needs, if only we express them correctly. The purpose of urban design is to change the status quo to leave the city better than you found it.

Urban designers do not design cities; they design the tools that change cities. Those tools are the products of urban design: discrete, actionable, and made to change the status quo. Those tools are rules, plans, and pilot projects that transform neighborhoods. They are only urban design if they are transformative.

Urban design operates at the intersection of politics, finance, and design. You can be the best designer in the world, but if you can't design under the pressure of politics and the stress of finance, you are not an urban designer.

In fact, nothing important in a city can change without an alignment of politics, finance, and design. The Interstate Highway System had been authorized politically in 1938 and designed at the Futurama exhibit at the World's Fair in 1939, but construction had to wait until 1956, when a financing mechanism, the gasoline tax, was put in place.[5] In climate change mitigation, you can have a market for emissions credits, you can have a design technology for renewable energy, but if you don't have a political mandate, you will have nothing but the status quo.

WHO SHOULD READ THIS BOOK?

The Nature of Urban Design is written for anyone who sees the need to transform our cities. This includes people who want to become urban designers, particularly students and practitioners in the field of politics, finance, and design who help to decide how a city will change. The book is also written for those people whose lives will be changed as a result of urban design; I want to give them a framework to participate in the process of change.

Many people realize a vague need for change in our cities, but they feel powerless when they are confronted by the enormous complexity, the lack of political transparency, and the high cost of even a small public project. This puts a barrier between those who change a city and those whose lives are changed. Whenever we hear of work going on in our neighborhood, we ask, "What are *they* doing now?"

I want people reading *The Nature of Urban Design* to realize that with a little information and the benefits of understanding the urban design framework change in cities, *they* can become *we*. Then the question becomes what do *we* want to change? Ordinary citizens can affect their city to a degree they may never have thought possible by becoming participants— stakeholders willing to take on a political, financial, or design role in the process of urban design. Where there currently is no bottom-up community input, we can demand it. Where there is a lack of top-down leadership at the executive level, we can replace it. The city is ours.

Whether that city becomes a just city as well as a wealthy city or a beautiful city is directly related to the degree of participation that its citizens

Young urban designers try their hand at drawing in Paley Park during urban design week in New York. *(Credit: Colin Gardner)*

achieve in its transformation. But what does participation mean when there are twenty million people in a city? What does participation mean when poor neighborhoods are walled off from their richer neighbors?

If urban design is such a powerful tool of transformation, why do some citizens live without toilets while their neighbors bathe in luxury swimming pools above them? I can only answer that a city is never finished, and urban designers need to work toward decreasing barriers to participation in shaping the city by increasing transparency in the urban design process. *The Nature of Urban Design* provides a road map to the urban design process to identify the maximum points of leverage at which participation is most important.

Although *The Nature of Urban Design* delves into examples that are unique and local to cities, particularly New York City, the readership of this book is global. There is something about urban design, perhaps its preference for drawings over talk-talk that makes it ideal for communicating, no matter what your native language. I notice this with my students and apprentices at City Planning. They come from all over the world to New York, and it is sometimes hard to communicate verbally, but those differences melt away when we draw. Urban design turns out to be a universal language, and I am proudly astounded that when we pin up our projects, we communicate with a degree of precision, creativity, and enthusiasm that is the very definition of fluency.

HOW TO USE THIS BOOK

Reading this book is only an introduction to reading something much more important: the city around you. To really learn about a city, to *read* a city, you have to walk it. So take this book outside and find a beautiful public space to read it. Draw all over this book to record how people are using the space; record important dimensions (there is a scale printed on the cover) and note details.

This book describes the purpose, the people, the process, and the products of urban design and puts its power in the contemporary context of rapid urbanization in an era of climate change. It is designed to have a lot of small details branching from a few big ideas. You can simultaneously develop an overall understanding of how to change cities while delving into a particular topic that resonates with you. Use this book to participate in the transformation of your city; you can leverage your involvement by understanding the process of urban design and target your effectiveness by knowledgeably communicating with people in other fields who may share an urge to change the city. If you are an educator, use this book for learning; the framework is a condensed course of study about urban design, and each topic can expand into much deeper inquiry when applied to real-world challenges facing cities today. Every city, every neighborhood, is different, so lessons learned from *The Nature of Urban Design* will never

produce the same product, but they will produce the same result: change.

Use this book to understand your city. When you learn how cities change and who changes them, you will begin to notice the marks of urban design in every stone and street. You will come to understand that what matters most is how people use civic space, how they live their lives together in cities. And you will learn that decisions made long ago resonate through the built fabric of cities to influence how we and our children will live our lives.

The Nature of Urban Design is prefaced with a personal experience. It is the story of becoming an urban designer by discovering one goal: to leave the city better than we found it. This introduction then lays out why we should care about cities, understanding that cities are great, cities are growing, but cities are vulnerable.

In the first chapter, I define cities and the urban design framework that changes them, setting the contemporary global challenge of growth during climate change. I consider how cities affect climate and how climate affects cities, and look at New York as an example of the transformative power of urban design. The second chapter looks closely at the process of urban design and how cities change, while the third chapter identifies the products of urban design and how each is used in changing the city. The fourth chapter combines process and products to consider how a contemporary urban design response, the High Line, transformed its neighborhood in New York. The final chapter places these tools in the global context, showing that if we want to make the world sustainable and resilient, first we have to make cities livable. I offer global examples and metrics to guide the transformation and conclude with a look at how my own neighborhood might adapt to the challenge.

If you are perfectly happy with the status quo,

don't bother with this book. This book is only for people who want to improve the way we live, which is increasingly happening in cities. I hope that if enough people read this, their eyes will be open to see how many like-minded people are around them. Barriers of profession, of status, of age can melt away when a common vision becomes evident. I believe there is a broad, shared ethic of sustainability in the world that is only now awakening, experiencing the extremes of criticism and boosterism, the birth pangs of both ridicule and overpromising. This is not so different from the stage that car culture was at during the World's Fair in 1939 when a Futurama model caught the attention of the population and set the stage for the massive suburbanization that began just over a decade later. We are at only a very early stage of sustainability; our task is to turn this ethic into built works that prove to ourselves that we have the means of accomplishing—and prove to our children that we have the hopes of achieving—a lasting, just, and bountiful life in cities.

AFTER THE STORM

Nine days have passed since the hurricane hit. My power is back on, but until last night I hadn't realized just how much of Red Hook, including the housing projects, still don't have power, or heat, or water. Before the time change last week, I had gotten home before dark. Last night, biking from Manhattan, I went through blocks and blocks of darkness, starting at the mouth of the Brooklyn-Battery Tunnel. My own block and a couple of others are a strange island, lit while all around us is shadow.

It was a scene of devastation. The streets were empty. Every five blocks there was a single light from temporary police units. The one light at the projects

was pointed up like a prison searchlight at the empty building.

As I turned the dark corner onto my block, something unexpected appeared. A pizza oven. A mobile pizza oven. It was surrounded by people, my neighbors, talking and laughing. They borrowed power from Fort Defiance, our corner bar and restaurant, badly damaged in the flood and still out of action. But the real warmth came from the coals in the metal barrel, which served as a pizza oven, and the faces of the volunteers serving.

Although our urban design thoughts normally go to bulk and land use and permanent things, tonight the most useful and lovely thing was evanescent. This pizza oven transformed what had become a dark and desolate corner after the storm into a lively community gathering place (and got me off the hook for getting home late and not having planned dinner). In an hour it was gone. But for that evening, it made the street the heart of the neighborhood; it improved civic life by improving public space.

The next day I faced the daunting task of finally cleaning out the ground-floor apartment in my house, which was totally destroyed by the flood. It was hard to face up to the task. The tenant had evacuated in time, but the place was a sodden mess. Mold and insects were taking hold. It's the sort of task that is so difficult you just resign yourself to never starting. But the doorbell rang. Volunteers. A group was forming across the street, they had secured boots and gloves and heavy-duty trash bags. They asked if they could help.

The entire day, wave after wave of volunteers came through. Some were my neighbors. Some came from other parts of the city. One man told me he couldn't in good conscience stay in his apartment, dry and safe in Brooklyn Heights, and think of other neighborhoods in need. Another man told me that he

was an actor from London who returned to help because on a visit five years ago Red Hook had reignited his love for New York and for the creative life of cities. So he put on a mask and gloves and got to work helping me.

Red Hook is normally a quiet place, but that day and for many days since, the streets—the public space—have been thronged with people participating in the cleanup. I have never felt prouder of a public space than I did the streets of Red Hook.

Our responsibility now is to change our city so the next flood will not be devastating. But we need to keep the sense of community that is our real resilience. To change our cities while improving the quality of public life is the nature and mission of urban design.

Volunteers bringing pizza to Red Hook, Brooklyn, after Hurricane Sandy. *(Credit: Alexandros Washburn)*

"While coming into being
for the sake of living,
the city exists for the sake
of living well."
—Aristotle

TOD is watching. *(Credit: Alexandros Washburn)*

CHAPTER 1

WHY SHOULD WE CARE ABOUT CITIES?

Cities are where we want to be. As Aristotle said, "While coming into being for the sake of living, the city exists for the sake of living well." The promise to raise our lives above mere existence to the plane of "living well" is the siren call of cities through the ages, and explains why cities have attracted an ever larger share of the world's population over the course of history. If present trends continue, more than two-thirds of us will choose to live in cities by century's end. Across the globe, we may complain of those cities as difficult, expensive, overcrowded, yet the attraction remains. Despite the hassles and challenges of urban life, all of us who have tasted life in cities know that what John Updike wrote about New Yorkers also applies to those who live in cities anywhere across the globe from São Paulo to Istanbul to Shanghai. "The true New Yorker,"

Every month, approximately four million people leave villages and countryside for the fringes of an already established city...

and by extension, the true urbanite, "secretly believes that people living anywhere else have to be, in some sense, kidding."

There is a wondrous attraction of cities, as powerful as our imagination. People so much want to live in cities that their migrations result in forming the equivalent of a city the size of Paris every month. But this is a woefully misleading statistic, which might suggest the monthly unveiling of a lovely new city with cafes, boulevards, art museums, and a great subway system. But the reality of rapid urbanization is nothing of the sort.

Every month, approximately four million people leave villages and countrysides for the fringes of an already established city. These cities grow by bursting at the seams, with sewers, if any, overflowing. In the fastest growing cities, which tend to be the poorest, little planning is done ahead of time. The new arrivals often meet danger and discomfort in what seems like an alien world.

Despite often deplorable conditions faced by new arrivals to cities, statistics show they have probably made the right bet if they are looking for a better life. As a measure of prosperity, the World Bank records economic density—the amount of economic activity that takes place in a given land area—and finds that it correlates with urban density. Cities are indeed the land of opportunity. Today there are just over three billion people living in cities. According to the United Nations, by 2050, there will be three billion more. Pulled by opportunity or pushed by destitution, the half of the world's people who don't live in cities but want a better life will move to cities to find it.

The population shift to cities comes with an uncomfortable corollary. People who live in cities as they are currently designed produce more greenhouse gases than people who don't live in cities—as a global average about three times more. More greenhouse gases, more global warming. More cities, more greenhouse gases. If current trends in urbanization continue and that growth is not managed sustainably, we're heading for an environmental catastrophe due to global warming. Or the possibility of disaster could be avoided. People in cities, particularly coastal cities threatened by inundation, are waking up to their vulnerability to climate change. They are also waking up to their responsibility. Cities affect climate and climate affects cities. This newly acknowledged responsibility is reflected in new trends in urban design, in newly conceived projects, plans, and standards that try to make cities more sustainable and more resilient in the way they are designed, built, and inhabited.

What does it mean to be "resilient"? The way we design our cities today is not resilient. This is easy to see in the sprawling suburban cities of America that consume fourteen times more energy per capita than the global average. But it is also true of the massive new cities of Asia that are built more densely, but squander the efficiencies of density by dividing neighborhoods with a checkerboard of impassible multilane highways. It is also true of the spectacular growth of the poorest cities in the world, where new neighborhoods are built on dangerous floodplains or muddy slopes without sanitation or other infrastructure. The urban design patterns of the status quo are inefficient, alienating, or unsafe.

Urban design could make cities resilient. A well-designed, well-built city could be the most efficient, safe, and enriching place on earth. It could be a place that can adapt to extreme weather with no more danger to its inhabitants from a storm surge than from a spring shower. It could be a place where the greatest creativity is applied to economic development, education, health, and art. It could be a place where even walking down the street is a spectacle. Resiliency today means living well in a time of climate change.

Cities are places of living well: Singapore pool 55 stories above the city.
(Credit: Alexandros Washburn)

As Aristotle hinted, cities are where people want to be. As mentioned in the introduction, cities take many forms, from tract houses in suburbia to skyscrapers downtown. Statistically, cities are not just downtowns, they are entire metropolitan areas that include every extreme of density and wealth. And they are very hard to define precisely. Though we have been building cities for more than five thousand years and more than two billion people live in them, there is no consensus definition of "city."

The United Nations, faced with many different standards of its member states, statistically throws up its hands and admits there is no globally accepted definition beyond a vague sensibility of "bright lights, tall buildings, and traffic jams." But this misses the full menu of urbanization.

In Iceland, 200 people living together gets you a city. In China, you would need 100,000 to qualify as one. In the United States, there are many statistical gradations that come together to make up the largest measure of city-ness, the metropolitan statistical area (MSA), defined as urban areas and their surrounding counties that have a high degree of integration with the core areas. The subcategories of MSA include urban fringes (unincorporated areas adjacent to urban areas), urban places (incorporated areas with at least 2,500 people), and urban areas (at least 50,000 people and at a density of at least 1,000 people per square mile. The broad variety of the U.S. statistical definitions of "urban" gets at the underlying principle that there are many morphologies of city today, many ways to design and live together, a complete spectrum from farmhouse to penthouse integrated socially, economically, and infrastructurally.

The morphologies of a city today can be as varied as the people who live there. New York is a prime example of the broad diversity in the form and feel of the city. Manhattan, home to the United Nations, certainly fills the bill for "bright lights, tall buildings, and traffic jams." But my remote corner of Brooklyn also feels like a city, with its old brick warehouses and crumbling docks. There are parts of Queens with suburban homes with driveways and carports. There is even a mobile home park in Staten Island, with trailers in neat rows with potted plants covering their wheel wells. The residents are all New Yorkers.

Yet hard as it might be for a citizen of the five boroughs to say this (you've got to be kidding if you live elsewhere, after all), the experience of the city extends into the region around New York City, crossing all manner of political and geological boundaries to form the New York Metropolitan Statistical Area. A shopping mall in New Jersey, an office park in Westchester County, a bedroom community as far away as Stroudsburg, Pennsylvania. These places would not have developed without the pull of the city. They are inextricably part of the urban network.

SIZE MATTERS

The diversity of experience available in cities makes them difficult to categorize statistically except by one simple measure: population. If you measure the overall population of their metropolitan areas, cities come in only three sizes: small, medium, and large. If you are in the majority of the world's population that lives in cities, you live in a city, a metropolis, or a mega-city.

New York arguably became the world's first mega-city when the population of its five boroughs and immediate suburbs passed the ten million mark in the 1950s. Since then, the number and distribution of mega-cities from Mexico City to Tokyo has become almost commonplace. Asia alone has a dozen such cities.

Before the rise of the mega-city, the metropolis was thought to be the most sophisticated form of city. With over a million inhabitants but less than ten million, the metropolis emerged in the nineteenth century from the wealth of the Industrial Revolution with a binary sensibility as both the city of squalor and the city of light. A metropolis such as Paris or London became the crucible of modern culture. Today, however, a metropolis is no longer the mark of empire. The best, such as Sydney, Australia, with a population of four million, are wonderful places to live, regional capitals of great beauty, diversity, and liveliness. These cities maintain their competitive edge through their connection to other cities globally and their quality of life locally. They try to find a sweet spot between mega-cities and cities.

Though the majority of the world's urban population will eventually live in mega-cities, the fastest growing and currently most common class of city is that with less than 500,000 people. These cities are at best subregional capitals, and their capabilities for planning and implementing the infrastructure of growth can be relatively weak. As their population grows rapidly, particularly in Africa, they will come under increasing stress with relatively fewer resources than their largest counterparts.

Density in Hong Kong.
[Credit: Alexandros
Washburn]

If we want to compare two global cities, the small, medium, large categorization is of little use. There is an infinitely fine grain to even the largest cities, so a comparison requires being quite precise about what you are comparing and the boundary across which you are comparing. Take, for example, a comparison between New York and Hong Kong. Which city is denser?

Density is a measure of how many people live within a certain area. Within their political boundaries, New York City and Hong Kong have similar land areas and populations: 469 square miles and 8 million people for New York and 426 square miles and 7 million people for Hong Kong. At that scale of comparison, the average density of the two cities is quite similar at around 17,000 people per square mile. But Hong Kong actually limits its built-up area to only 100 square miles, leaving three-quarters of the land as public parklands or public rights-of-way. New York leaves one-quarter of its land for parks and streets. Squeezing similar amounts of development onto less land means the average density of Hong Kong's built-up area is about 71,000 people per square mile, almost triple New York's. Hong Kong, therefore, must be the denser city.

But wait! If you calculate the density of Manhattan, New York comes back out ahead at 83,000 people per square mile. Hold on, if we limit ourselves to Kowloon in Hong Kong, then we are talking about 117,000 people per square mile. And so on. It all depends on where you draw the line.

BOUNDING

Where you draw the line is called bounding. The easiest boundary to apply to a city is its political boundary, such as the line that surrounds New York's five boroughs. Political boundaries are often historical remnants; New York's reflects an expansion in 1902 but does not take into account any growth since then. Given the tremendous growth of the last century in most cities, for almost any contemporary urban data we may wish to sample, the political line significantly under-bounds both the essence of the city and the influence of a city on its region. To make meaningful comparisons on economic and social and demographic data, you need to be able to sample a city at several different scales, to draw the boundary at different places. That is why the U.S. census doesn't rely only on political

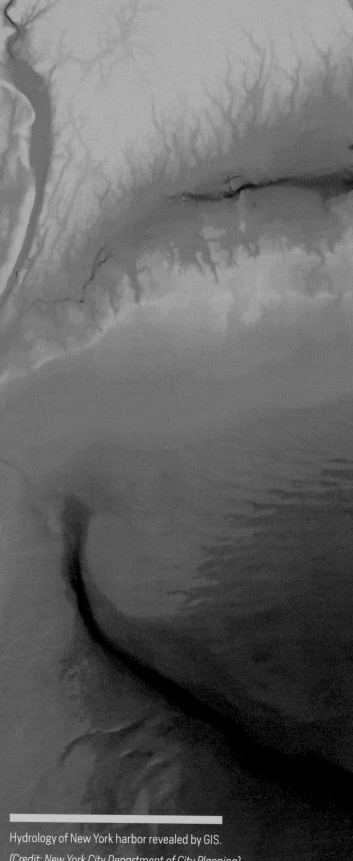

boundaries, but instead uses finer-grain divisions called census tracts and then aggregates them into an MSA, which, in the case of the New York MSA, crosses the political boundaries of three states and hundreds of municipalities.

The choice of boundary, as we saw in the comparison of New York and Hong Kong, is critical for an honest comparison. And within each boundary, the choice of variable to be sampled is similarly critical. In trying to define what a city is, metrics and intuition, boundary and variable, must be made visible.

The complexity of a city can not be addressed with a single variable, such as population density; in fact, there is no limit to the variables we can use to describe a city. These variables could reflect what we care about in a city. They could be demographic variables and sample ethnicity or education levels or income; they could be infrastructure variables and sample sewer capacity or transit speed; they could be cultural variables and sample schools, museums, performing arts centers.

The accuracy of mapping has improved considerably through modern techniques of satellite imagery, laser radar, and building information systems so that a boundary can be drawn at almost any scale. The city of Sydney is working on a project to map not just the function of every building, but even the function of every *room* in the city.

But the true revolution in mapping is the ability to accurately associate diverse information to points in space through geographical information systems (GIS). With the prevalence of information via the Internet from sources as diverse as city databases to Flickr pages, just about any characteristic about cities can be quantified as a variable. Through GIS, the information can be associated to a map, whose modern resolution can essentially allow bounding at any desired scale.

Hydrology of New York harbor revealed by GIS.
(Credit: New York City Department of City Planning)

The visualization afforded by GIS is stunning in its ability to translate raw data tables into images. In preparation for the New York City Comprehensive Waterfront Plan, we took a data table of water depths in New York Harbor and mapped this in different shades of blue using GIS to show the bathymetry of New York Harbor as a continuation of upland topography. The resultant image is exceedingly accurate but also revelatory, a new way to see the city as one with its waterways and watersheds.

Eric Fischer (https://twitter.com/enf) is one of the most creative users of GIS, creating data tables from social media. His map of geo-tagged tweets in New York paints an alternate set of rivers to the ones we mapped—rivers of people passing through the city. When they are impressed by what they see, their exclamations are recorded as tweets and mapped.

The newfound latitude in mapping of choosing any descriptive variable and setting any appropriate boundary is of immense help in creatively defining a city. In essence, it gives you a set of quantitative metrics that can be applied to both quantitative and qualitative variables. The water depth data points in New York Harbor are quantitative variables. The "oh my!" tweets of a visitor entering Times Square are qualitative. But both can now be mapped with extreme spatial accuracy through GIS. Because a city is a place of emotion as well as fact, aspiration as well as achievement, the ability to track both quantitative and qualitative data is an invaluable tool for urban design.

With so many variables to sample and statistical comparisons to be made, urban designers can mine the complexity of the city for actionable information, looking for dependent variables. If you change one variable, how will it affect another?

Using one variable, such as population density, and one boundary, such as the political border, is never enough to define a city. The reverse is true: every variable and every boundary that can be visualized uncovers a new city layered on top of the one we thought we already knew. Just as there is a political New York, there is a health care New York, a cultural New York, a culinary New York of delicious ethnic complexity. We can map it. There is a commuter's New York, a grocer's New York, even a raindrop's New York in which we map the rivers and their watersheds. These many cities have different boundaries, and these boundaries may be fluid over time, adjusting in and out with rush hour or nightlife, but they all are real, palpable, mappable, measurable in some fashion. Each city exists simultaneously with the others, boundaries overlapping. We each keep mental maps

A raindrop on its journey.
(Credit: Skye Duncan)

of whichever set is important to us. This allows us as citizens to navigate the multiplicity of our city's functions and the mix of its messages. We hold these maps together in our unconscious, layered and overlapping, called forward from time to time by duties, appetites, hopes, and longings. The many New Yorks held within us pulsate in our imagination like a beating heart. Now as urban designers, by spatially mapping the many parameters of this dynamic, multiplied city, we can record and perhaps anticipate the very next beat.

Statue of Liberty.
(Credit: Alexandros Washburn)

THE CITY IS PART OF NATURE

The misconception that suburbs are not city is entangled with an even greater misconception: that cities are not natural. Cities are a part of nature, they are the habitat of our species. Cities are subject to the laws and whims of nature as much as any other patch of Earth.

Historically, we have thought of cities as apart from nature. Originally, coming together to live behind a wall in a city was a form of protection from the wilderness. We did not wish to be eaten while we slept. Fair enough—one could see how a division between urban and natural might be comforting. But as we grew in population and then in our ability to exploit natural resources after the Industrial Revolution, our attitude toward nature took a curious reversal. We no longer thought of ourselves as vulnerable to nature. Instead, we realized nature was vulnerable to us. With some sewage from nineteenth-century New York pumped unfiltered into the harbor, we could kill off mammoth oyster beds that had fed generations of inhabitants. With a hunger for lumber to build our houses, we could raze entire forests. With a desire for central heating, we could choke the air with coal dust and acidic rain would fall. We became a menace to nature and to ourselves, and began to write laws to curb the worst of our excesses. A century ago in the United States we created a national park system to preserve land from development and keep it apart as nature. A half century ago, we passed the Clean Air Act and the Clean Water Act to protect nature from our pollution. We had come to realize that in being a menace to nature, we had become a menace to ourselves.

In the swing from protecting ourselves from nature to protecting nature from ourselves, we institutionalized a division between man and nature that has clouded our thinking. Each of these two extremes is a form of paranoia. Neither extreme is sustainable.

The design of cities—urban design—is the field where we will first see defined a new relationship, if we can achieve it. Our success in managing our cities will parallel our success in managing our environment. Nature and the city are one.

The interdependency between cities and nature needs to be quantified to be believed, especially because the paradigm goes contrary to centuries of tradition and law that posited nature as separate from humankind. With global warming, rising sea levels and the increasing frequency of storms like Hurricane Katrina and Hurricane Sandy, it is becoming more obvious that cities affect climate and climate affects cities.

We are going to have to shift from a paradigm in which either man or nature is victim to one in which we acknowledge our interdependence and design the management of that relationship into the form of our cities for mutual benefit. To do so successfully requires an understanding of the relationship between cities and climate change.

HOW CLIMATE AFFECTS CITIES

Climate change affects all cities with a combination of extreme events and chronic conditions for which they are not physically or socially prepared. Hurricane Sandy was an extreme event, and its effects on New York were acute and devastating for those of us in the path of its storm surge. The rising level of water in New York Harbor is a chronic condition and its effects may be less dramatic, but they will be more pervasive.[1]

Before Hurricane Sandy, we used to ask if New York was prepared for "the big one." We didn't want what happened to New Orleans to happen to New York. The effect of Hurricane Katrina hitting New Orleans in 2005 was a glimpse of how much havoc extreme weather can wreak on a city, even a well-established metropolis in the strongest, richest nation on Earth. The image of bloated bodies floating across streets was a shocking image of the damage a climate event can do to a city.

We made computer models of hurricanes hitting the New York region, and my associate Thaddeus Pawlowski even made a computer model of a fictitious but realistic New York neighborhood we called Prospect Shore to test the impact of a modeled Category 4 hurricane strike and our ability to recover.[2] When Pawlowski ran the simulation, the result was 695,000 homes destroyed, 1.2 million people homeless. We began to make contingency plans and a playbook for emergency housing. In 2011, we had a near miss with Hurricane Irene. In 2012, Sandy hit. Now we know the effects of an extreme weather event.

Residents in cities across the globe are coming to learn the chronic effects of climate change. It afflicts cities not only with catastrophes, but with daily operational challenges. Increased temperature, more variable precipitation, and higher winds are becoming a fact of urban life. And all this against a backdrop of constantly rising sea levels as rising temperatures increase the rate of polar ice melt. As sea level rises, coastal cities will find more of their population closer to sea level, or even below it. Rotterdam is an example of a city familiar with the dangers of too much water and too little elevation. It doesn't take a perfect storm to threaten the city's everyday viability.

Rotterdam exists because of its access to the water. It is Europe's greatest port, situated at the delta formed by the Rhine and Meuse Rivers on the North Sea. And although not picturesque like Amsterdam, it has a strong wharf-like sensibility to its landscape and architecture. If you take a water taxi, you will nose around the tugboats and find a place to land on one of the quaysides. To reach the buildings, you have to go up over a levee first. The levees are part of an enormous infrastructure of sea gates and pumps the city must maintain along with a command and control mechanism to open and close them at just the right time. This infrastructure is necessary because Rotterdam is largely below sea level. It rains frequently—nobody lives in Rotterdam for the climate—and there are strong tides.

In the recent past, there has been increased precipitation, and as a result, the water table has risen and left the land with little ability to absorb more water during a storm. Storm water must therefore be channeled away from the land and into the North Sea. However, when the storm is coming off the North Sea, a storm surge builds up head, and the city must close its sea gates to protect itself. But it can't keep them closed for long. Not only can't the ships, on which the economy depends, go in and out of port, but if the gates are closed, then how do you drain the storm water out to sea? Meanwhile, the Rhine and Meuse Rivers are bringing billions of gallons of water toward the city from their watersheds over a large swath of Europe. As the tide goes out and the river water descends, the sea gates must be opened and then quickly closed. Water is coming at Rotterdam from all sides, from the sky, from the sea, from the river, and from the ground. Rotterdam must literally juggle water to survive.

For other cities, the problems that climate change brings are not too much water, but too little. Atlanta, Georgia, a major city in the normally rainy American Southeast, came within days of depleting its municipal water supply in 2008 after a prolonged drought.

Heat waves are becoming both more common and deadlier. The materials that cover much of the city—concrete and asphalt—trap this heat. When the sun goes down, streets and buildings are still radiating more heat. Hotter days and warmer nights put the population at risk of heat exhaustion, respiratory illnesses, and increased outbreaks of diseases. For many people, especially the elderly, the homebound, and those with special needs, air-conditioning becomes like life support.

The combination of chronic climate changes in a city can also produce unforeseen second-order effects. Atlanta has a very hot, muggy climate in summer, and during the drought, water was diverted from watering plants and used to run air-conditioning, exacerbating the heat-island effect of the sprawling city. The combined drought and heat-island effect led to a "downtown tornadic event," the first time in the city's history that a tornado touched down in the urbanized center.

Greenhouse gases are invisible, but you can "see" how a city produces them if you take a walk down the street and observe closely the everyday activities and settings of urban life. In New York City, you can see this in how people build, manage, and use buildings—the biggest emitter of greenhouse gases. To be precise, 78 percent of New York's total emissions comes as a result of burning or transporting fuel to heat, cool, light, and power our buildings. How those buildings are built and operated makes a difference. You can see the building built in the 1920s with thick walls and operable windows, which could make it very energy- and hence carbon-efficient, but it still uses its original boiler, burning bottom-of-the-barrel fuel oil. If it switched to natural gas it could cut its emissions in half. No quick fixes for the building built in the 1960s, though, with single-pane all-glass facades. And this may be the biggest energy hog on the block, if the lights are still on inside even though everyone has left the office to go home. As a side note, many of the leases are written with the tenants paying for the electricity, and the landlord adds a surcharge to the electrical bill, creating an incentive for the landlord to keep the building inefficient.

You can not walk around New York without seeing a new building under construction.

You can not walk around New York without seeing a new building under construction. You may see a builder putting on a new facade with insulation, a rain screen, and high-efficiency windows. The builder may be increasing density too, and mixing uses by making the ground floor commercial with housing above or offices above. With advanced lighting and climate controls, this building will use very little energy compared with its peers; therefore, this building is going to emit maybe one-third the greenhouse gases that the old one did. In New York we could easily achieve our 30 percent carbon reduction target by rebuilding to modern standards. Unfortunately for our overall average, new buildings and substantial renovations are still the minority of the building stock. Even though it seems there is always a crane working in sight, 80 percent of the buildings that we will occupy in New York City in 2030 have already been built.

Bubbles on a New York City street showing the percentage of carbon emitted by various sources.
(Credit: Alexandros Washburn)

Tomorrow is trash day in New York City, and people are leaving their garbage and recyclables on the sidewalk. Our trash, such as the empty container of out-of-season blueberries, which had to be flown in from Chile, represents the emissions from our personal consumption. Picking all that up and sending it to landfills has a significant impact on the carbon dioxide emissions bottom line: in addition to the transport, refrigeration, and disposal truck emissions, an additional 2 percent goes to "fugitive gases" such as the methane that eventually is released as the garbage decomposes in a landfill. Eating local and composting would help here—for instance, buying produce from Brooklyn Grange, which converts industrial rooftops to farms.[3] An acre of rooftop can produce about 15,000 pounds of fruits and vegetables in a year, along with several hives worth of honey.

On the positive side of the ledger, New York's street trees are sequestering carbon dioxide out of the atmosphere and storing it in their trunks and leaves, thus reducing our carbon footprint. London plane, Norway maple, and Callery pear are the top three varieties. Each tree can absorb almost fifty pounds of carbon dioxide from the atmosphere every year (http://www.ncsu.edu/project/treesofstrength/treefact.htm), in addition to providing shade in the summer to reduce the cooling load on buildings and making it delightful to walk down the street in any weather.

New York is the most efficient big city in America because of its transit. Only 7 percent of the already low transportation-related carbon emissions of New Yorkers comes from the subway, even though the subway is our dominant mode of transportation and it moves the equivalent of almost an entire population of the city every day—seven million people!

The subway has another benefit for keeping our carbon dioxide emissions low; it also allows us to build densely. If I look up as I walk down Court Street in Brooklyn, I will see twenty-story buildings clustered near the subway stop. This is an example of transit-oriented development, a policy New York has followed for more than a century in which you put density near the subway stops so that people can combine walking with a subway ride to reach home, shopping, work, or leisure.

When it comes to how cities affect climate, there is no need for metaphors, you just count emissions. New York has a full-time employee who does nothing but count carbon. Add it all up and it is called New York City's carbon footprint—49.3 million metric tons of emitted greenhouse gases.

New York is learning fast from the disaster of Hurricane Sandy. We are learning both that we have an enormous amount to do to become resilient and that urban design can play a decisive role in our transformation to resilience. As we look to other cities for lessons, best practices, and experience, we are also coming to see how much we are like other cities in the world. We might like to think we are exceptional, but we share the challenges and opportunities of hundreds of other cities in the world.

We are a coastal city, and almost a half million of our citizens are in the path of flood and storm surge. We share the challenge of making these neighborhoods safe with the coastal cities across the globe, and particularly with the more than six hundred million people living within a meter of sea level.

We are a diverse city, in every measure reflecting cultures from around the world. Ethnically, we are a broad mix, and we live in a mix of building typologies from skyscrapers to trailer homes. We live in neighborhoods ranging from the densest urban canyons to lawn-edged suburban bungalows. We are comfortable with our differences.

We are growing, as are other great cities in the world. We expect a million more New Yorkers in the next generation. We are great in our aspirations, and feel the same eagerness for tomorrow that every growing city does. And things happen fast in New York. We can have an idea, an urban design idea, and if the stars align, we can see the results in a decade.

We are a laboratory for building and living in cities. And like it or not, we are in the crosshairs of climate change. We have extremes of hot and cold weather, and we are in the path of hurricanes. We look to other cities for ideas, from sea walls to bicycle paths, but we test ourselves on whether we can make them real. Our experiments in resilience become models for others; though we are exceptional, we are somehow also prototypical.

New York is a model for urban design because, as the song goes, if you can make it here, you can make it anywhere. New York is a crucible for change. It presents the highest impediments and the greatest rewards. So it might benefit our understanding of the nature of urban design to study briefly the history of urban design in New York and the transformation it has brought about.

A BRIEF HISTORY OF URBAN DESIGN IN NEW YORK CITY

A history of the urban design of New York City might begin with the Dutch, who established the fortified trading colony of New Amsterdam on the island of Manhattan in 1609. The Dutch urban design tradition is a long one, and they are considered today to be among the world's top planners, rational and dogged in their pursuit of sustainability.

To which I enjoy telling my colleagues in Holland, "The last time New York was sustainable was before you showed up." So let's begin a short urban design history of New York not with the Dutch, but with their predecessors, the Lenape Indians. The Lenape had occupied Manhattan for hundreds of years before the Dutch arrived, and through a gradual process of landscape management using fires and nonlinear patterns of cultivation, they had created fifty different ecosystems—call them neighborhood habitats—on the island. We have a very precise picture of what their version of the city—which they called Mannahatta—looked like because of the work of Eric Sanderson, a biologist with the Wildlife Conservation Society. Sanderson calls cities "habitats for humans," and he combined his training in ecology with

Manhattan then and now. New York from the time of the Lenape Indians to the present as recreated through the scientific work of Eric Sanderson. *(Credit: Markley Boyer/The Manhattana Project/Wildlife Conservation Society)*

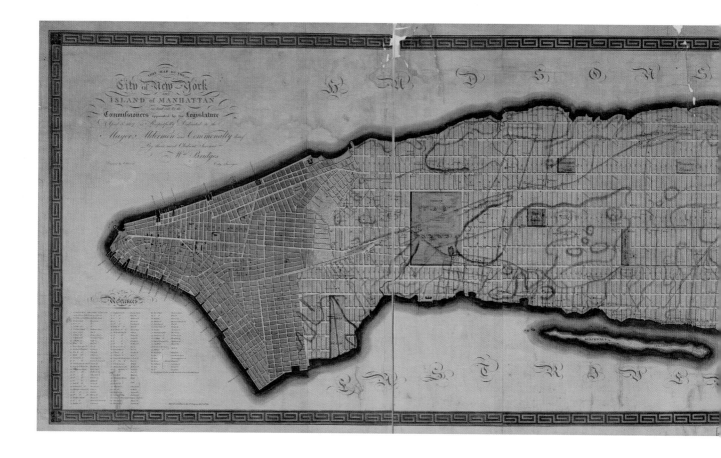

sophisticated mapping techniques to produce a three-dimensional model of the island circa 1609.[4]

Using the oldest, most topographically accurate map of the island available, a map the British military produced in 1782 to place their defenses during the Revolutionary War, Sanderson combined satellite photography and geographic information systems to accurately place all the island's natural features, locating Lenape settlements at their statistically most likely points along the island's waterways and clearings. He then used biological data of species relationships and preferred habitats to produce a Muir diagram—a map of the relationship showing which animals, insects, and plants required which other animals, insects, and plants as part of their daily life in their habitat. Sanderson counted almost one thousand species in Mannahatta at the time of the Lenape stewardship. The Lenape landscapes, which he can map to the accuracy of a city block, varied from meadows to forests to clearings with groupings of huts, in which, Sanderson likes to point out, the Lenape crowded themselves in more densely than did the Lower East Side immigrants in their tenements three centuries later. New Yorkers, it seems, have always been partial to apartment life.

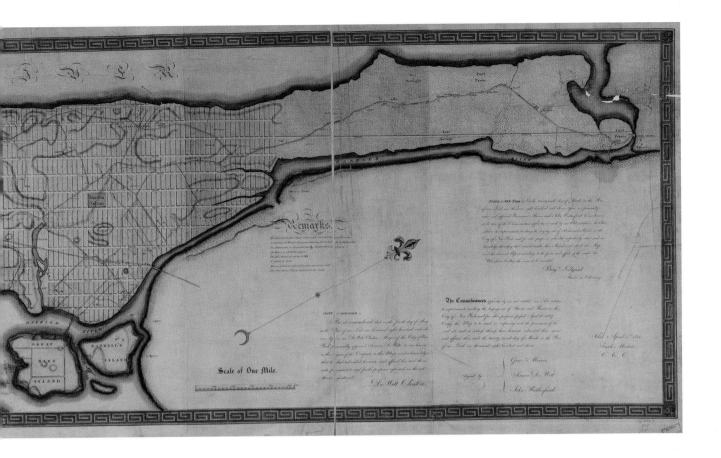

The commissioner's grid mapped onto Manhattan, 50 years before Central Park changed the face of the island. *[Credit: Library of Congress, Geography and Map Division. Map created by William D. Bridges.]*

Fast-forward past our colonial era under the British to life in the new United States, where New York was determined to surpass its rival Philadelphia as the largest city in the nation. In 1811, a group of New York City commissioners drew a plan to erase the last remnants of cultivation by the Lenape or the early Dutch settlers. They mapped the complete transformation of Manhattan by a dense grid of streets that, if built and occupied, would make New York larger than any city in the world.

The commissioners of 1811 eschewed the whimsy of contemporary town planning with its roundabouts and radial avenues. They chose a grid because they thought it more economical. The grid awkwardly spliced into existing neighborhoods like Greenwich Village's meandering streets and skewered through to Lower Manhattan with an extension of Seventh Avenue, one of several new one hundred foot–wide avenues going north-south. The cross streets were sixty feet wide and spaced two hundred feet apart, a pattern that provided more than two thousand blocks for real estate development.

The commissioners did not anticipate a need for public open space. "It may, to many, be a matter of surprise that so few vacant spaces have been left, and those so small," the commissioners wrote in the report

My three bosses: Fred, Jane, and Bob. In every project we do, we need the nature of Frederick Law Olmsted (a), the quality of Jane Jacobs (b), and the quantity of Robert Moses (c). *(Credits: (a) Painting by John Singer Sargent; (b) Photo by Maggie Steber; (c) Getty Images)*

accompanying their plan. But when the price of land is "so uncommonly great," why set aside room for "vacant spaces"? The commissioners wanted as much land as possible for the tax rolls and suggested that the public could satisfy its need for open space by visiting Manhattan's shores instead, along the two broad rivers that embraced the island.

Around 1840, Cornelius Vanderbilt began buying land along the shore of one of these rivers, the North River, or, as we call it now, the Hudson, to build a freight railroad up the west side of Manhattan. At the time, friends wondered why he would build a railroad in such a sparsely populated area. "Put the road there and people'll come" was his answer.[5] Perhaps Vanderbilt, who got his start in business operating sail-powered ferry boats, recognized the industrial potential of the Hudson River shore of Manhattan after the visit of the first steamship to New York in 1838. Sailing ships couldn't beat against the tide upriver and therefore docked downtown, but Vanderbilt recognized what the commissioners never could have imagined—that steam power, when applied to ships, meant that all of Manhattan's shore would be accessible to commerce and valuable for docking.

Not having anticipated the steamship, the commissioners did not map the waterfront as public and so protect it by law. As a result, by the latter half of the nineteenth century, industrial development became most intense along the shore and made recreation impossible. Manhattan bristled with docks. The waterfront was closed off to the public and the adjacent upland serving its industries became almost infernal.

Lumberyards, brickyards, lime kilns, gas houses, glue manufacturers, swill-milk cow stables, freight yards, stock houses, and slaughterhouses filled each lot. A smoke-belching locomotive slowly pulled freight down Commodore Vanderbilt's Tenth Avenue railroad preceded by a cowboy on a nag to shoo away pedestrians. The entire public realm appeared to be a factory.

Social ills and disease began to multiply. Tuberculosis was rampant. Gangs such as the Gophers and the Parlor Mob prowled Manhattan. The Tweed Ring dominated politics and turned a blind eye to the crime, producing neighborhoods like the "Tenderloin," a place of such concentrated vice that a cleric complained, "the prostitutes outnumber the Methodists."

For the ordinary citizen of mid-nineteenth-century Manhattan, there was no relief from the ills and press of the city, no public space large enough or green enough to catch your breath with your family on your one day off. If you wanted a moment of quiet and a patch of grass, your best option was to visit a cemetery.

Frederick Law Olmsted

This story of midcentury malaise needs a hero, and for me it is New York's first truly great urban designer, Frederick Law Olmsted. Olmsted gave us Central Park. He recognized the capacity of nature to solve infrastructural and social problems while improving the quality of urban life, and he had the canniness to make his vision a reality.

Olmsted operated at a time of spectacular urban growth—in percentage terms, greater than our own. He was a landscape architect. He knew only enough of politics and finance to ensure that his designs would get built. He was neither a man of the people nor a master of the universe. But he succeeded in transforming New York through Central Park more thoroughly than any mayor or tycoon.

He was practical and held no illusions about the power of design relative to the power of politics and finance. The design of Central Park was brilliant, but the decision to build it was a wrenching political and financial wager made in a money-mad city hobbled by corruption and influence. The wager was huge: 848 acres of developable land to be taken off the tax rolls, three thousand lots of real estate to be bought and paid for at public expense, and then the formidable sums for the landscaping of the park itself, which no one could properly estimate because no American city had ever undertaken to build a park of this scale. The arguments were fierce, and Central Park almost did not get built. The fact that its lawns and rambles were engineered to also include a reservoir necessary to solve the city's water problems eventually tipped the debate in its favor. Olmsted's art was well served by his engineering.

The wager of building Central Park of course paid off, and in retrospect it would be hard to imagine the growth of New York into the capital of the twentieth century without Olmsted's grand achievement of Central Park in the nineteenth century.

Robert Moses

In the mid-twentieth century, in the era of Robert Moses, New York came to be the largest city in the world, not just the largest city in America. Moses

> *The wager was huge: 848 acres of developable land to be taken off the tax rolls.*

was not a designer or a financier or an elected politician, but I consider him among New York's greatest urban designers for the sheer scale of his accomplishment. He was an appointed official who spent his entire career in government. You could call him a bureaucrat, but that title doesn't fit someone who had amassed such control over the system of building in New York that he was known as the "Power Broker."

He had begun his career by building parks, using his genius for getting things done to bring light and air to some of the poorest neighborhoods in Manhattan. He went on to improve the ragged edge of Manhattan's Upper West Side, bringing the public back to the waterfront by making a chain of parks and a parkway leading downtown. He slung a new expressway across Brooklyn and Queens that broke into three levels to hide itself beneath a promenade on Brooklyn Heights. He built an elegant new headquarters for the United Nations on the site of a former stockyard.

Moses turned out projects of unprecedented scale, but, increasingly, of questionable purpose. Using federal "slum clearance" dollars, Moses acquired sites that were hardly slums, evicted the residents through eminent domain, razed their homes, combined the city blocks into superblocks, and then built hundreds of nearly identical cruciform towers to house what he hoped was a new middle class. He always favored the automobile in his projects and banned subway lines from the rights-of-way of his roads. He built bridges connecting his expressways and then tolled them, using the proceeds to back an issuance of bonds to build yet more projects. He was unstoppable.

At the pinnacle of his power in 1958, Moses found his Waterloo in Greenwich Village, where he met the most unlikely Wellington: Jane Jacobs, a self-described housewife with big glasses. Moses wanted

to enlarge a road through Washington Square Park. She organized her community. She stood her ground. She won the battle. And with a grant from the Rockefeller Foundation, she wrote *The Death and Life of Great American Cities*, opening the door for a new wave of small-scale, community-based design to counter the heavy-handedness of top-down urban planning.

Jane Jacobs

Moses had perfected top-down management to increase the scale and capacity of the city in record time. But the constant change under Moses—the sheer quantity of his interventions—had bred a wariness in New Yorkers. The quality of life in the city was felt to be slipping, even as Moses's infrastructure and building statistics kept leaping ahead. The city was at risk of losing the quality that made it worth living in. "New York is a city no longer in love with itself," wrote one journalist. But the quality

that had been lost in Moses's metropolis, Jane Jacobs found at her doorstep. She showed New Yorkers how to rediscover the fine-grain quality of their daily urban lives, and in so doing to create a revolution in their neighborhoods. For this, she is my third great urban designer of New York.

Jane had moved into a modest Greenwich Village row house with her young family just after World War II. The house on Hudson Street still stands amongst a row of shop fronts, with the White Horse Tavern at the end of the block, where she would often repair for a pint of beer and conversation with her neighbors. She knew every shopkeeper and every family in her neighborhood, and they knew her. Hudson Street was the laboratory for her book. It was on Hudson Street that she developed her theory of the necessity to have "eyes on the street" to maintain a sense of community and public safety. Those eyes needed something to look at, and in a healthy neighborhood, the informal social interactions played out on the street provided the attraction. The rhythms of daily life she called "the ballet of Hudson Street," and she realized that her Village neighborhood had come to mean almost as much to her as her family itself. That sentiment persists in New York, where a recent poll found that after their families, New Yorkers love their neighborhood best.

Jane Jacobs rediscovered the quality in New York City streets; her neighborhood tavern, the White Horse Tavern, remains a center of informal community ties.
(Credit: Alexandros Washburn)

Our twenty-first-century urban design agenda differs from past eras in that everything we must accomplish must be achieved against a backdrop of climate change. The first urban design challenge New York faces is population growth within existing boundaries. We are expecting a million more New Yorkers in a generation. To provide homes and jobs, we have to use the land we have more intensely. If you overlay a map of the New York City subway system, our strategy becomes clear. We have up-zoned near transit stops and down-zoned in areas served only by cars. Our increased density comes on top of our transit system. This is called transit-oriented development, or TOD. Although other cities may be just now waking up to its virtues, New York has practiced TOD since the first subways were built a century ago. TOD is New York's DNA.

The second urban design challenge is resiliency, and it's a two-fold challenge. The immediate concern is to protect the city from the weather events and sea-level rise that are already occurring as a result of climate change. The more long-term test will be to reduce carbon emissions from

the city to decrease future global warming. We have 573 miles of coastline to protect and an emissions reduction target of 30 percent to achieve by 2030.

The final urban design challenge for New York City is to succeed at the first two agenda items while simultaneously improving the quality of life in the city. The technical solutions we find would be wasted if they failed to improve public life, which we equate to improving public space. Examples to inspire us are everywhere from Central Park to Paley Park. In chapter 4 we examine how a new inspirational urban design project, the High Line park, transformed the West Chelsea neighborhood around it.

To succeed in our twenty-first-century urban design agenda, which is to grow our population, to become more resilient, and above all to improve the quality of public life, we need to follow the lessons of our three greatest New York urban designers. We need to achieve the quantity of Moses, the quality of Jacobs, and the nature of Olmsted in every project we design.

Density in Kowloon, Hong Kong.
(Credit: Alexandros Washburn)

Sandy at night. *(Credit: NASA Earth Observatory image by Jesse Allen and Robert Simmon, using VIIRS Day-Night Band data from the Suomi National Polar-orbiting Partnership [Suomi NPP]. Suomi NPP is the result of a partnership between NASA, the National Oceanic and Atmospheric Administration, and the Department of Defense. Caption by Michael Carlowicz.)*

Opposite page: Cities are a place of living well: Budapest fountain. *(Credit: Skye Duncan)*

View of the Bronx River. *(Credit: Alexandros Washburn)*

Sunset from the Brooklyn Bridge. *(Credit: Alexandros Washburn)*

Opposite page: The Chicago Loop.
(Credit: Alexandros Washburn)

A sign appearing around the West Village. *(Credit: Douglas Moore)*

More Jane Jacobs Less Marc Jacobs

Times Square edge.
(Credit: New York City
Department of City Planning)

Street Walls in Manhattan (Top: E. 17th Street;
middle: E. 18th Street; bottom: West 87th–88th Streets).
(Credit: New York City Department of City Planning)

CITY PLANNING COMMISSION
DEPARTMENT OF CITY PLANNING
22 READE STREET
NEW YORK, N.Y. 10007-1216

CHAPTER 2

THE PROCESS OF URBAN DESIGN

T he products of urban design may differ in every era, but the process stays the same. It is a kaleidoscope producing maddeningly complex patterns from the overlap of three not very transparent forces: politics, finance, and design.

When a city's pattern of growth eventually threatens its well-being, compliance becomes counterproductive, and urban design must come to grips with its own failings, now revealed in the excesses of the previous pattern, and begin anew. Pattern, repetition, flaw—how could it be otherwise? We are human, after all. But there is no time now to brood over past mistakes or to settle old scores. The future dwarfs the past. Urban growth today is upon us at a scale greater than the world has ever experienced, and we need transformation faster than we can produce it.

Sketching out the process of urban design. When I became chief urban designer, I realized I needed a framework to explain to others how the process of urban design works. *(Credit: Alexandros Washburn)*

The process of urban design has responded successfully and quickly to threats in the past. When the spread of infectious disease through the tubercular tenements of the Lower East Side threatened the health of New York City in the 1890s, someone had to ask: how can we change the design of the city to stop the spread of disease? New building and sanitation codes and new water and transportation systems determined through a process of urban design allowed New York to continue to grow while removing the threat that one out of every two New Yorkers would die of infectious disease.

Today the question for urban designers is what are the specific rules, plans, and projects that will transform how a city is built and that will allow it to grow sustainably? The urban design process is the path to answering those questions. As with any design process, urban design features a repetitive cycle of observation, analysis, and representation. However, unlike other design processes, urban design is done under constant pressure from the forces of finance and politics, which turn every decision into a struggle. Even seemingly simple questions such as "where is the site?" and "who is the client?" demand extensive negotiations, consultations, and bargaining. At the end of the struggle, the process of urban design results in the products of urban design: a visualization of a desired future, which is codified as rules, adopted as plans, and built out through exemplary pilot projects, which set the pattern for a new wave of business as usual growth. When the new growth pattern is established as the model, the process of urban design returns to being mainly a check on compliance . . . and the cycle continues forward until the next crisis, hopefully a long, long time hence.

No important change can take place in a city without an alignment of politics, finance, and design. Politics is the greatest force in determining what gets built; politics takes many forms in the urban design process. It can be top-down authoritarianism, à la Robert Moses, or it can be bottom-up community activism, à la Jane Jacobs. Whatever the form of the political decision making, nothing can happen until a decision is made, because politics decides how public resources will be used, who will benefit from a change, and who will pay the bills. Even withholding a decision is a form of political power. A wise old bureaucrat once told me, "True power is not the power to say yes or no; it is the power to say nothing at all." By delaying decision, a government can starve a promising prospect or exact a dreadful concession.

Likewise if the forces of finance are ignored, there is no hope of implementation. A successful financial model is the transformational trigger that allows repetition of the elements to form the eventual urban design pattern. Finance is what allows elements to "scale"—to multiply small units into a greater whole. It is the process that turns a fractional penny for a single Internet ad into a multibillion-dollar corporation such as Google. Repetition via a successful financial model is the scalable engine that drives the build-out of urban design decisions. The same repetitive process turned a few pennies of gas tax into the Interstate Highway System beginning in 1953. The interstate highways of America, though authorized by Congress, had been languishing for twenty years before a financial system, the gasoline tax paying into the Highway Trust Fund, was devised to get the highways built. The financial system was so successful that there was no stopping the sprawl once it began. Every time we bought a gallon of gas, more money would go into the Highway Trust Fund, which would pay for more roads to be built, which we used to drive more, which means we bought more gas, which put more money into the trust fund, which built more roads, and on and on. With the system complete, flat consumption, and no appetite for increasing the gasoline tax, we now face the reverse situation: disinvestment as the roads show their age and we can't afford to maintain them, let alone build new infrastructure. Scaling can also apply to buildings, the profits of which can be applied for making streets on which to build more buildings and make more profits. Such was Baron Haussmann's technique for building the boulevards of Paris through his financial system, the Crédit Foncier. The construction of boulevards and the transformation of the streetscape of Paris ended only when the Crédit Foncier itself became bankrupt and the financing ran out.

Compared to politics and finance, design is always the weakest force in determining whether a project gets built. Moreover, in the process of urban design, the window of opportunity for design opens only briefly. When politics decides on a course of action and finance figures out a way to make money at it, there is little time left for design changes. The window shuts and the frenzy of building begins based on the plans at hand.

The urban design process is always in a state of tension with politics and finance: though a weaker force, urban design is by definition a long-term enterprise, and therefore must challenge the assumption of compromise in politics and the profit motive in finance, both of which tend to the short-term. By always seeking to put transformation in a larger context, urban design plays the necessary role of helping a society see the forest for the trees.

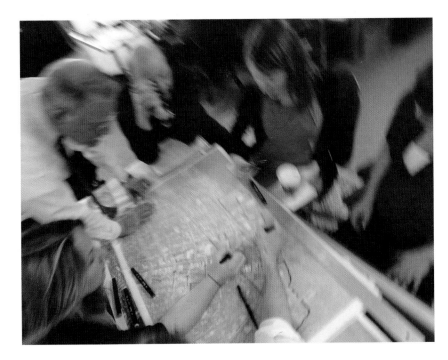

Urban design at the center.
(Credit: Alexandros Washburn)

What is the recurring process of urban design that produces the ongoing physical transformation of cities? The process is maddeningly complex, iterative, and nested. It is complex because it operates at the intersection of politics, finance, and design. It is iterative because urban design requires a cyclical application of the processes of observation, analysis, and representation. And it is nested because it operates differently at different scales, requiring the application of a consistent point of view to translate basic design values from the scale of the sidewalk to the scale of the city.

The process of urban design is a struggle to decide the form and function of the future city that will sustainably accommodate a changing population and shifting demographics while increasing resilience. The decisions reached through the process of urban design are a reflection of the values of the city's people, their hopes for living well measured against the challenges of their era. Because of the slowness of the city-building process, the hopes for transformation embedded in the urban design process are often realized only later, for the children of those who make the decisions and generations to come. The goals of the design are often at odds with the short-term nature of the election cycles of politics and the desire within finance for a quick return. However, the success of the urban design process must be judged not just formally and in retrospect, but contemporaneously by how it affects people's personal welfare, their sense of belonging to society, and ultimately the health of the neighborhoods in which they live.

Many urban designers, myself included, begin their careers as architects. As architects, we are actually at a great disadvantage. It is a virtue for an architect to be rational, logical, and demanding in their work—to be a "control freak." Yet being a control freak is an impediment to good urban design. The worlds of politics, finance and—at the scale of a city, even design—are not within the architect's control. But they can be within the architect's influence. To control nothing but influence everything is an attitude that characterizes the urban design process. In trying to exercise control over a solution that integrates politics, finance, and design, the detail-oriented architect sometimes misses the most important point: designing the question can be more important than designing the solution. (More on this later.)

Client, site, and program are all quite clear in architecture: a client is the one who pays, a site is the land on which the building will stand, and the program is the spaces the client wants the building to contain. There is no such clarity in urban design. Who is the client? Is it the government? The community? The owner? Outside stakeholders? What is the program? Is it what a private developer wants? What a community group wants? Or is it something no one wants—such as a waste treatment facility—but which benefits the entire city? And is the site a particular piece of land that a client controls, or is it the area the project will affect? Alternatively, can the site be nullified, as those who oppose a project using a "not in my back yard" argument contend? Every one of these questions involves a struggle, and the urban design process has to somehow make sense of it all.

At best the process is supple and can adapt quickly to new information or to an alignment in political or financial incentives. At worst, it is an endless feedback loop in which the action is studied to death and nothing ever happens. Some people have made entire careers producing a series of urban design studies and environmental impact statements on a project, and retired well before there is any hope of implementation.

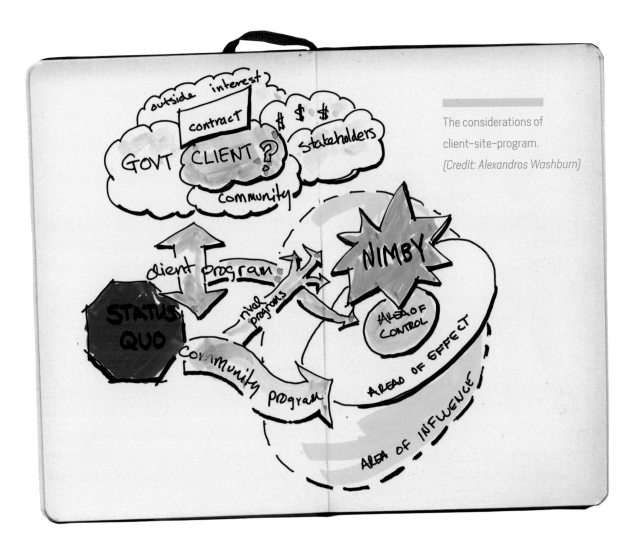

The considerations of
client–site–program.

[Credit: Alexandros Washburn]

DESIGNING THE PROBLEM

The urban design process can be broken down into three phases. The first
I like to call "designing the problem." It starts with an urban design study
that describes existing conditions and poses a series of questions to clarify
the forces that will determine site, client, and program. The purpose of the
first phase is to state the problem properly. The purpose of the second phase
is to design the solution to the problem. (It should be obvious that no amount
of talent can produce the right answer to the wrong question, but human
nature cannot resist jumping to solutions.) The third phase in the urban
design process is the implementation of the proposed solution, in which
those putative products of urban design become real. Plans are adopted,
rules are enacted, transformational projects are funded and built. If those
tools are successful, the city will change, but it will be at the hands of others. The urban designer has completed his or her work with the completion

Pedestrian is judge.

(Credit: Alexandros Washburn)

Therefore, the urban design study can be thought of as a proper statement of the problem. At its best, it provides an informed vehicle to negotiating questions of client, site, and program.

Who Is the Client?

The client is the one in charge. In urban design, the client isn't necessarily who pays the bills. The client is the person or entity the urban designer must serve and can be a jumble of stakeholders, from the city itself, to government entities, private interests, not-for-profit groups, community associations, even disadvantaged individuals who may not have a voice. All are stakeholders with varying degrees of say in the process.

- Government—whatever its ideology—is supposed to operate in the interest of its citizens, and so government is the obvious client for an urban designer. Yet "government" is quite difficult to define because any ruling system usually includes geographic layers (national, regional, and local, at least) further subdivided into functional departments (environment, transportation, parks, planning, etc.) with often overlapping jurisdictions and competing agendas among its leaders. New York is famous for its competing jurisdictions and tangle of community, city, state, and federal powers. Singapore, by contrast, seems a model of clarity.

  The Singapore Urban Redevelopment Authority (URA) has a stable political mandate, ample state resources, and enormous power to shape the built environment of the city-state. With the minister of national development at its head, the URA is a cabinet-level organization in charge of the country's most precious resource: the small amount of land within its

of the tools. I say this to counter a seductive fallacy. Urban designers build the tools that build the city. They do not build the city itself.

The process of urban design begins by asking a series of questions and negotiating their answers. The urban design study (phase I) is equal parts observation, analysis, and representation. The study can take many forms, from a highly researched publication to a series of informal conversations. The study is not neutral because it is conducted, like all else in urban design, under political and financial pressure. It should frame the question of what exactly is being transformed and why it is being transformed.

borders. The URA follows a policy to increase density while increasing the intensity and diversity of the nature within its borders. The present chief executive of the authority is Ng Lang, who previously served as the city's parks commissioner. The authority includes within it a department charged with increasing the quality of urban design and architecture, and streetscape is given its own department. Some view this as a model of efficiency but wonder if it can be a model elsewhere; most other cities have state and federal governments above them to meddle in their affairs and, as in the case of New York City, to gather in taxes far more than is returned in aid. In Singapore, the city is the state, a model that the historian Fernand Braudel would applaud. Singapore houses its people, grows its economy, and acts on its plans in a way few other cities in the world can do.

• **Community groups**—I find that local community groups are often the best informed clients in urban design. They are small enough to know the individual needs of their members, and—when they are well organized—can stand up to government. In Kibera, Kenya, an otherwise disenfranchised neighborhood found the power to change its environment by forming a community group to rectify a problem the government wouldn't address: raw sewage in their neighborhood. Because the government would not put in sanitation infrastructure, they organized to collect their waste in composters, package it, and then sell it to farmers as fertilizer, using the profits to build a soccer field in the floodplain where the sewage formerly rotted.

An urban designer should value highly the input of local community groups while understanding that any diverse community may spawn one or more such groups, sometimes competing and in opposition to each other. Parsing their message, weighing their needs, and reaching consensus in a community through urban design is as much art as politics.

• **Institutions** such as hospitals, universities, and any other large organizations carry substantial weight as stakeholders. They are chartered to operate in the public good, but they have bottom lines and clear self-interest. Often they will seek approval for expansion, put pressure on public space or building density, and face opposition from neighbors. The important civic functions that institutions provide and the public or semipublic spaces they create are difficult to weigh but essential to maintain.

• **Private developers** are often agents of change. They come in all different scales, from builders of individual homes to international corporations that build megaprojects. What they have in common is that they unify control of land, financing, and design for their own benefit or the benefit of their investors. The projects they produce may also be in the general interest of the city, but not necessarily so. A private developer will seek to maximize profit. It falls to government planning agencies to harness that profit motive for the greater good—as New York City organized the air rights transfer to save the High Line park—or rein them in. Where the government fails, community groups and, occasionally, the courts fill the void.

What Is the Program?

The program is the list of objectives that a project must meet, a list of functions for which a plan must provide space. Stakeholders argue about program, and it is necessary to understand the negotiating positions of each if the urban designer seeks to be an honest broker in reaching a compromise. Wading into these shark-infested waters may be dangerous to the continued employment of an urban designer, but program matters to urban design. For instance, if too much building is programmed for a site, there may be too little public space. Typically, revenue-producing elements of the program, such as housing or commercial building space, are oversupported by paying clients. Non-revenue-producing elements of the program, such as schools and sidewalk amenities, typically have much less political and financial support because they cost money and don't immediately provide a return. Yet they are essential for a sustainable city. Complex decisions on walkability and the incorporation of green networks can get short shrift if the urban designer does not stand up for them by communicating that these non-revenue-producing elements are in everyone's long-term interest, including the private developer's. It is the urban designer's job to insist on a proper accounting for the public good.

When negotiating the program, the urban designer needs to be able to consider quantitative questions in relation to qualitative goals. "What are we transforming and why?" is a precursor question to "Should we include a supermarket and how big should it be?" If we program for a regional-scale supermarket in a rezoning we are planning for the Bronx, we would get an

immense one-story building behind a sea of parking. That might maximize the number of grocery jobs, but would it transform the neighborhood? If, instead, our aim is to turn an impoverished tract of subsidized housing and vacant lots into a mixed-use, mixed-income transit-served neighborhood, then we want a medium-size grocery with limited surface parking that would also be accessible to those without cars in the neighborhood and could act as an anchor to increase the walkability of the neighborhood for more transit-oriented development.

Urban design can broaden participation in the process of program analysis to nonprofessionals by showing the community and the stakeholders the physical implications of each program option. For instance, if you want to make a street function better for pedestrians, you need space for the functions that make walking a pleasure. But the space in the right-of-way is finite. Ample sidewalk, clear paths, adequately sized tree pits for healthy roots—these functions take space from other functions such as parking or automobile travel lanes. Further, urban design can articulate core values of public space that support a preferred programmatic option. Urban design can

then help negotiate among the stakeholders, parsing needs from wants as each program option is sketched out and battle lines are drawn. But at some point, the political process makes a decision on the program, for better or worse, and the designer must work within those limits.

Where Is the Site?

The site is where the project goes. For architecture, the concept of site is clear: the site is a piece of land that the client controls and on which you put your building. But for urban design, whose purpose is larger-scale transformation, the site can not be limited by narrow considerations of parcel ownership. Just as urban design has a constituency broader than an individual client, it has an effect larger than a particular parcel of land.

Transformation, once ignited, rarely stays within the boundaries of site control, and so urban design must anticipate the extent of transformation and its intended effects, both immediate and long-term. This question translates into a definition of site in three parts: the *area of control*, the *area of effect*, and the *area of influence.*[1] All three boundaries must be negotiated. People will fight to be included or excluded, depending on what they perceive to be the effect of the contemplated urban design action on their specific land, their neighborhood, and their overall relation to the city. The process of urban design can visualize for the stakeholders these three scales of site boundaries and help clarify the intentions of the transformation.

The *area of control* is the narrowest definition of site for an urban design process. Ownership by the client of legal title to the land in the area of control is one way of defining the boundaries of the area, but such homogeneity of legal control is rare in broad urban design projects. The operative quality that defines the area of control is the ability to make decisions about land use, infrastructure, and resources within those boundaries. The decision-making ability means that the area of control is the area that can be most completely transformed by the urban design project and in turn can become the springboard for the transformative effects of the project on the other two larger scales.

In many cases, legal title does not exist. The favelas of Rio are easy to bound by looking at their building typology of shanties and borrowed infrastructure, but they are extremely difficult to bound based on land ownership or tenancy, because many of those living there are renting from earlier favela dwellers who never perfected title. Yet the neighborhood residents are the clients, and improving the health of the favelas is critical to improving the health of the city.

Given the relative expense and scarcity of urban land, and the importance of land ownership and consent in the normal process, the area of control is rarely larger than a few blocks for the typical urban design project. On occasion an urban designer will have the opportunity to work on an entire neighborhood, and in rare instances an entire new city. When the site is a greenfield, and an entirely new city is being planned, having an area of control as large as a city somehow hollows out the process. The rancor of existing stakeholders gives texture to the solution, and entirely new cities risk the dullness of homogeneous consent.

The *area of effect* is the next larger scale for analysis, defined as that area beyond the site that can or will change in explicit response to changes at the site. Often, the area of effect is called the "study area" in the urban design process and correlates to the "impacted areas" of an environmental impact statement. Intuitively, the area of effect can be considered to be the neighborhood. "There goes the neighborhood!" When a change occurs on a certain parcel of land, citizens care about how it affects their neighborhood.

The boundaries of the area of effect should be

characterized by measurable changes due to the urban design proposal. If you can't measure the change in some environmental, economic, or social variable, you are probably not in the area of effect.

The largest and most subjective scale of site is the *area of influence.* In taking an ecological approach to urban design, one could argue that the area of influence should be considered to be the globe itself. After all, if we are seeking to reduce local carbon emissions, we are seeking to affect global climate change. Yet one should be careful about how far to take the analogy. Everything is connected to everything else in urban design; a lack of discipline in prioritizing relationships at the largest scale will lead to analysis paralysis for even a seasoned urban designer.

The area of influence can also be envisioned as

the level where the neighborhood relates to the different infrastructures of the city. For instance, a new affordable, low-carbon housing development built on a parcel of land (the area of control) may positively affect the neighborhood (the area of effect), but how will it affect or be affected by the area of influence? What is the districtwide sewage capacity? How does the development affect permeability in the watershed? How does it map to the transit network?

The paradox of the area of influence is that is has different geographic boundaries for all these different infrastructures. For instance, if the urban design project included a vertical farm,[2] one could analyze the influence on food supply chains that extend well beyond the neighborhood. If the project were near a transit stop, an appropriate area of influence would be a map of the extent of the regional transportation system. To date, defining the area of influence has involved cataloguing qualitative relationships between changes in the area of control and their effect on larger-scale systems in the city.

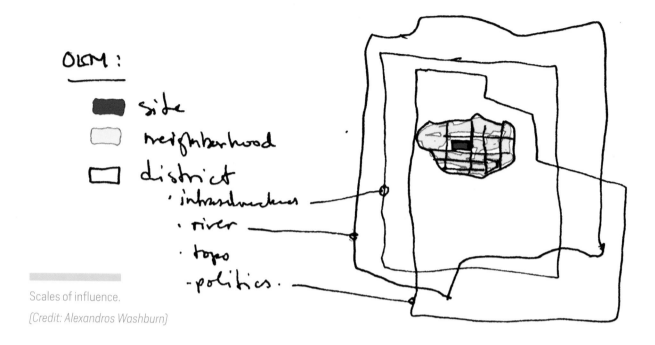

Scales of influence.

(Credit: Alexandros Washburn)

However, thanks to geographic information systems software, our mapping abilities for areas of influence are becoming quantitative. This has remarkable implications for sustainability and managing growth during climate change. An extreme example is the attempt to calculate the "ecological footprint" from everything consumed as a result of a project, from a cup of coffee to a yard of concrete, and thereby estimate the effect of the project on the carrying capacity of the earth's resources. Because climate change is the biggest challenge facing cities today, and because climate change operates at a scale far beyond the neighborhood, the process of urban design will increasingly be judged by how well it works at the largest scale of site, the area of influence.

Before entering a discussion of the second phase of the urban design process, I want to make one final appeal for the primacy of the first. I believe in the saying that *the worst, most corrupting lies are problems poorly stated*. If an urban designer has asked the wrong question, he or she will get the wrong answer, no matter how good the intentions, no matter how skilled the technique.

DESIGNING THE SOLUTION

The "solution" in urban design is expressed as a product of urban design: a rule, plan, or pilot project that sparks and guides urban transformation. The process of designing the solution is done in constant collaboration with community and under constant pressure from the forces of politics and finance, but the scope is far narrower than designing the question. We are seeking to create specific, actionable products. Designing the solution in urban design involves applying the exact same process as designing the question—observation, analysis, and representation—except that in designing the solution, there are laws to follow, votes to be taken, money to be raised, environmental impact statements to be filled out, and if we are ultimately successful in the implementation phase, a series of metrics to apply to see if this was the right solution, after all.

Over and over again in both designing the question and designing the solution, urban design utilizes a cycle of observation to see, analysis to understand, and representation to communicate what has been learned. This design cycle is common in the arts, but only in urban design are its products vetted and voted on publicly during the process itself, raising the stakes and extending the timeline.

Observation, analysis, and representation can not be separated linearly; they often occur at the same time in the same media. For instance, to observe a square, an urban designer might draw the space. But the act of drawing is a form of analysis, because certain details are included, others left out. The resultant sketch is a record of observation and a representation of what is learned. The drawing translates the thought process of the urban designer into a sketch form that others can see and thereby draw conclusions about what transformation is envisioned and why.

A complete process of observation, analysis, and representation can never be accomplished in a single sketch. More often than not, it takes months of data gathering, measurement, and the construction of a complex model to produce a vision. The process can be beguiling—what could be more interesting to an urban designer than drawing, pondering, communicating? Yet the point of the cyclical process is not to prolong the process itself—it is to produce discreet, actionable products such as rules, plans, or projects that can spark a transformation.

We need to observe how those habitats behave in relation to natural forces.

Observation

The second phase of urban design, like the first, begins with observation. Observation is a lifelong attitude of wanting to understand more about where you are. It may seem obvious, but observation requires being in a place. Although we can gather enormous amounts of information about a place off the Internet, there is no substitute for visiting in person, and while there, observing.

Observation is first and foremost about how people act in a space. William Hollingsworth "Holly" Whyte, the great New York urbanist, made a career of observing how people behave in public space, using stop-action photography, hand sketches, and field notes. Jane Jacobs observed the life on the street around her home in minute detail, particularly her own daily interactions with her neighbors, cataloguing what she called "the ballet of Hudson Street" in her book *The Death and Life of Great American Cities*. Jan Gehl's dictum, "first life, then spaces, then buildings" is a good hierarchy to guide the process of field observation.

Before beginning work, an urban designer should get a feel for a place by walking it. The human dimension, the sense of the history and the ecology of a place, can only be perceived by being there. The sum total of impressions about a place, even an ineffable sense of its destiny, is called the "genius of place."

When done well, the process of urban design doesn't just capture the genius of place, it transforms it. Urban design is dangerous because it can destroy the genius of place in the process of transformation. Therefore, an urban designer has a responsibility to understand the genius of place before acting. It is quite a responsibility, and an urban designer must navigate between extremes of timidity and callousness in the proposals for change. The least he or she can do is make an honest attempt to understand the genius of the place before changing it.

Observance of natural systems in relation to cities will tell us more about the city's place in the environment than any textbook, and the observation of natural phenomena will hold the first clue as to how to design a new generation of public space.

Eric Sanderson, biologist with the Wildlife Conservation Society, calls cities habitats for people, subject to the same relations documented in the Muir diagrams that describe other animal habitats. We need to observe how those habitats behave in relation to natural forces, for example, the process of rain falling, pooling, and coursing down urban arteries as people interact with each other and their urban surroundings.

In summary, observation—careful, critical, and sustained—is the touchstone of the urban design process. As urban design faces unprecedented challenges in accommodating growth during climate change, I am confident that there are solutions to be found in the spaces we already have and in the character of the people and ecology that animate them, if only we observe carefully enough, with new eyes to see familiar places.

Observing is not a passive activity. It requires making inquiry, recording results, and integrating what we experience somewhere in our memory for inspiration later. Sitting down and drawing what you see is the best method I know to really observe. Although a camera is an important tool in the hands of an urban designer, an overreliance on snapshots makes the observer a mere tourist.

Drawing is, in my experience, the best way to truly understand a space. Drawing, for an urban designer, is like reading for an author. It has nothing to do with how well you draw—some people can draw like angels, some resort to stick figures and awkward perspective. The act of drawing forces

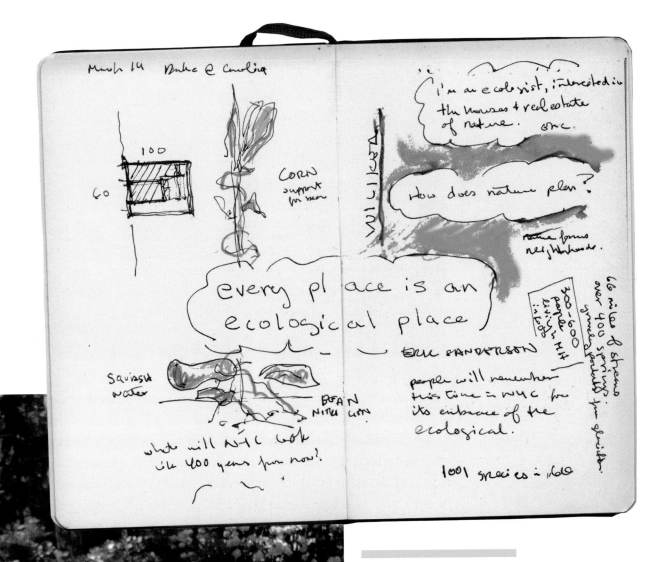

Every place is an ecological place.
(Credit: Alexandros Washburn)

If it is worth remembering,
it is worth drawing.
(Credit: Alexandros Washburn)

careful observation and a degree of critical thinking in deciding where to put the next line; the act of drawing forces you to filter and prioritize what is important about a place. Though critical faculty may operate subconsciously in a swirl of ink, the bottom line is that taking the time to draw forces you to look, and by looking, you learn. That is what I mean by observation.

If a place is worth remembering, it is worth measuring. A measuring device is an indispensable tool in observation, and as long as you record dimensions in a sketchbook, the device need be nothing more obvious than the length of your stride as you walk across a square. There is a ruler on the cover of this book for more precise measures. Use it. A camera is also a measuring device. If you know the dimension of one element in a picture, say the height of one story in a building facade, you can extrapolate most other dimensions in the picture.

I emphasize dimensioning as integral to observation because the success of a public place can depend on just a foot more or less for a sidewalk. By observing the dimensions of spaces you love, you will come to recognize commonality in certain critical dimensions. You will then be prepared to advocate and defend similar public space dimensions when they are challenged later in the design process by opposing interests.

Ultimately, it is the life in the space that you want to get to know. This requires little more than a "hello." People love to interact, and by talking to them an urban designer acquires many new sets of eyes with which to see the space. Shyness is rarely a barrier if you are drawing; people will always come up to see what you are sketching.

TOP DOWN

CITY PLANNING COMMISION>> COMMUNITY BOARD >> BOROUGH PRESIDENT >> CITY COUNCIL >> MAYOR

BOTTOM UP

Urban design includes many, many conversations. The purpose of these conversations is to engage the community and enrich the design, formally or informally. The New York City Uniform Land Use Review Procedure is an elaborate, legislated form of dialog, an outgrowth of the bottom-up Jane Jacobs movement in reaction to the top-down Robert Moses regime that preceded it. Until the 1960s, the urban design process in New York City was for decorative purposes only. The real decisions on the future shape of the city were made by a small group of men and carried out without regard to community input. Robert Moses was the Power Broker, and I have a vivid image of his "process" handed down to me from my mentor, Senator Daniel Patrick Moynihan. In 1956, Moynihan was a young aide to New York's Governor Harriman; it was his job to carry the great man's briefcase and to make sure there was scotch present. This meant that Moynihan was always in the room. He told me how Moses and the governor would meet. Moses would write the names of projects he wanted approved in pencil on a manila folder and hand it to the governor. That was it. Any further discussion, public or private, was for show.

The present situation in New York City is a good balance, an improvement on the manila envelope. There is a balance between autocracy and populism. The bottom-up movement is legally empowered to be heard through the land use review process, while the top-down structure retains the power to set the agenda of what comes before the planning commission. There is a dynamic tension between the quantity of Moses and the quality of Jacobs. I value the results as being better than either side could have come up with separately; however, the process results in a very long series of meetings with stakeholders, community groups, regulatory boards, the press, other agencies, advocacy groups, and many others who just want to be included. Everything may have been said, but if everyone hasn't said it, the meeting is not over. In urban design, not only does it help to be talkative, it helps to be patient.

Visual Representation

Representation in urban design is the technique of communicating a vision. Typically an urban design idea is represented as a series of drawings: plans, sections, and sketches accompanied by summary text, rules, or guidelines, along with a perspective illustration from the pedestrian point of view and some sort of physical model. More rarely, representation can also be entirely textual, like Jane Jacob's writing, or it can be virtual, taking advantage of advanced software and the Internet. Generally, urban design relies most heavily on visual communication to define a goal, and verbal communication to achieve it.

How you present your project is how you imagine your project, and an urban designer should strive for fluency and clarity. It is far better to be honest in your presentation with simple hand sketches that help you achieve fluency in making your argument than to apply a veneer of the latest computer graphic fashion. Students are particularly susceptible to fads, such as sexing up their computer-generated perspectives. Whether they are trying to illustrate a nightclub or a day-care center, the same Photoshop models seem to proliferate. Professionals, too, can be accused of the same veneering, working under immense commercial pressures.

Because urban design is part of a long, slow process of city building, judgments can't wait for the final product. The choice of representation technique is critical in urban design because it is not the eventual

The human aspect of drawing creates more accessible designs for public engagement than those that are computer generated, but both are necessary. The rezoning plans for Coney Island use: (a) a photo of existing conditions, (b) a sketch overlaying a computer-generated massing, and (c) a hand-worked sketch of the computer-generated graphic. [Credit: New York City Department of City Planning]

transformation that will be judged, but the technique that you choose to represent it that will be judged. An architecture critic can judge the merits of a built work, but an urban design critic must judge the merits of a rule, a plan, and only occasionally a built work. This puts special pressure on the representation of the project, and it is the mark of a seasoned urban designer that they will pare back their presentation to the form that most clearly expresses their ideas and

the argument that led to those ideas. More often than not, this comes down to the eloquence of a hand-drawn sketch.

Imagination in urban design is required both to ask the right question and to find the right answer. Imagination is called for daily and at every scale, yet each imaginative decision has practical repercussions that spread out like ripples from a drop of water, requiring testing and thought for the impact on the rest of the system.

Every designer has his or her own way of integrating imagination into the urban design process. I have found that drawing people, following natural process models, studying infrastructure systems, and applying intuition based on experience with precedents are the basis for my imagination. If I had to analyze further, I would say that allowing elements of these to recombine in daydreams and sketches and conversations with my colleagues is what leads to both a better statement of the urban design question and a better solution to the problem at hand. Perhaps that is what stirs the imagination most: a rapt consideration of the problem at hand and the support of your colleagues to experiment.

Precedents

What is observed in the process of urban design is called a precedent. It is typically a place, such as a public square, but it can also be a system, such as a zoning code. The best precedents are built precedents, not merely proposals, because built precedents can be visited and therefore judged personally. Built precedents have within them the accumulated wisdom of modifications, and built precedents contain working connections to the city around them, connections that help reveal the systems underlying the functioning of the precedent.

I find precedents are overused as inspiration and underused as a check on new designs. "This new street will become the Champs Élysée of the Borough of Queens!," a consultant breathlessly proposed as he unveiled his plans to build on the old ash pile of Flushing. I would rather have seen actual plans of the Champs Élysée overlaid onto his own plans, with a critical analysis of differences in the sidewalk depths, street widths, planting patterns, transit access, adjacent building bulk, solar orientation, grading, and any other category of comparison that would serve to illuminate whether the new street would function at all, let alone displace Paris. A lot can be learned from the details of the Champs Élysée, as well as from the Rambla (Barcelona), the Campidoglio (Rome), the Forbidden City (Beijing), or any great public space in the world without pretending that the original can be recreated.

Which is not to say that people haven't tried. Peter the Great took the precedent of Venice as the

starting point of St. Petersburg. He spared no expense, brought in Italian architects and stonecutters, dredged canals, even subsidized opera singers to make his new capital the equal of La Serenissima. The result is wonderful, but it's not Venice. In more recent times, the moguls of Las Vegas have taken another shot at recreating Venice in the desert of the American Southwest. They have also tried to recreate bits of New York and Paris.

Extreme examples as beautiful as St. Petersburg or as bizarre as Las Vegas prove that no matter how hard you try to plagiarize in urban design, you will not succeed in making an exact copy. When you copy a plan in a different place, you are only transplanting the roots of an urban design, not the results. The place itself will grow in its unique way over time. This would suggest that the process of urban design comes from the adaptation of precedents to local conditions. The High Line, for instance, was based in concept on the Promenade Plantée in Paris, a project that also turned a disused elevated rail line into a linear park. But the two neighborhoods have developed completely differently.

The futility of making exact copies in city building would also suggest that formal originality has little bearing on creativity in urban design. The grid of streets cast upon Manhattan by the planning commissioners of 1811 is dull and repetitive. Yet their plan, with changes over time—most notably the insertion of Central Park—has grown into one of the world's most dynamic urban designs.

La Rambla, Barcelona.
(Credit: Alexandros Washburn)

The best precedents are built precedents.
[Credit: Alexandros Washburn]

So precedent users beware: you can't copy success by copying a plan, but you can use the process of observation and analysis to find the critical criteria that translate to your project. The first, most important engagement with precedents is to identify ones that would be useful and to visit them, in your own city or abroad. Precedents, good and bad, are everywhere.

While observing and documenting, you should be asking how does the precedent connect into the networks and systems that support it? If you look at the Chrysler Building, a great precedent of architecture, get beyond the stainless steel spire. Follow the brick facade down to portals of the triangular lobby, see the magnificent murals on the ceiling but also look below where a stair descends in black basalt treads to the subway. Thousands pass up, through and out from multiple train lines, and the Chrysler Building stands rooted like an immense tree in New York's transportation network.

How does the precedent fit into the ecology of the neighborhood, both social and environmental? The new High Line park has gathered much praise for its reintroduction of native flora and fauna to the ecology of Manhattan. With the social popularity of the new park, the fauna now includes the peacocks of fashion who stroll and preen alongside the pigeons.

Although the ethos of a precedent can be recorded with sketches and photos, and its connecting networks catalogued loosely, the dimensional characteristics of a precedent have to be strictly observed. With the advent

erected. The best use of precedents is temporary and supportive of contemporary goals. The urban design product may bear as little resemblance to its precedent as an arch would to its framework. The framework is taken away, and the arch stands on its own.

So why depend so heavily on precedents for urban design and not rely instead on the artistic creativity of an individual designer? The answer is probably best put in the old Latin phrase, *ars longa, vita brevis.* Art is long; life is short. Artists have lives measured in years; precedents have centuries to develop. Their forms reflect stores of accumulated information on successful urban function over time. Their dimensions mark the framework that supports the interaction of countless systems. The best incorporate a pedestrian point of view that has stood the test of time.

As Nikos Salingaros, the mathematician and urban theorist, has pointed out, the best precedents often have gone through a process of accumulated, random change that over time has increased the complexity of the system in a way that no rational development could foresee.[3]

Particularly in urban design, which seeks transformation over time, it is very difficult if not impossible to predict all the ways a space will be used, and how then that space will adapt to those new uses. Precedents have been through that process the long, hard way. If they succeed, they enter the canon of great public spaces, like the Ginza in Tokyo, the Rambla in Barcelona, or the Grand Bazaar in Istanbul. They become precedents as much because of how they work as how they look. Embedded within their forms is a record of minutely adapted function that is a storehouse of empirical evidence for the contemporary urban designer.

How can precedents help us solve the unprecedented problems of urban growth during global warming? Dealing with global warming requires a

of Google Earth and the availability of dimensioned satellite photography, overall dimensions are now extremely easy to generate, display, and compare.

Because of the limited resolution of satellite photography, more detailed information may require site measurement. Dimensioned plans, and most important, dimensioned site sections, give the crucial information about how a space is divided among its users and how the space interacts with the buildings around it, and the sun, rain, wind, and topography. In a detailed site section you can put a person in for scale and begin to understand site lines and sequences of perception. To take it a step further, if the precedent seems particularly promising in relation to a new urban design, you can make a three-dimensional computer or physical model and generate perspectives and overlays to critique the new plans and compare connections.

Urban design's goal is transformation, to build a bridge from the status quo to the future. Precedents are often the scaffolding on which that bridge is

Facing the charrette.

(Credit: Alexandros Washburn)

complete rethink of the way we build cities. Precedents are records of success (and failure) in urban design. The question is how to maintain success while mitigating and adapting to global warming; the answer is to add new variables and new dimensions to the equation. Cities are marvelously adaptable to new functions. If those new functions are to create food, to create energy, or to create land in a way that leads to sustainability and resilience, then precedents will provide the framework to integrate those functions while protecting the vibrancy of human-scale urbanism.

Collegiality

The urban design process is a highly social, highly collaborative art. It depends on collegiality and the belief that we are working toward a common purpose, and requires respect for the opinions of others. Collegiality is expressed in the urban design process through goal setting with principals in politics and finance, design charrettes with the community, peer reviews with other professionals, and interdisciplinary collaboration with experts in the fields that touch on urban design.

A charrette is an intense public work session, a direct design engagement with the community. There are many methods of running one, but the essential agenda is to present the urban design site and program to a meeting of stakeholders and treat them as clients. The stakeholders, guided by a team of facilitators, often break out into smaller groups to draw and discuss solutions. At the end of the charrette, typically less than a day, the entire group reconvenes, reports, and synthesizes its results.

An urban designer guides a charrette with a statement of values. Entering the charrette, a designer should be prepared with two things: a point of view about what's right, and a willingness to hear what's wrong. Both the designer and the community should learn something through a charrette, building up trust in the process, but the goal is to discover shared values and make them explicit in the design.

The peer review process adds professional insight. It is a collegial process in which planners, designers, and others responsible for similar urban designs get together to criticize and improve the work at hand. At the Department of City Planning, all projects go through both formal and informal peer review, internal and external. The Policy Committee members are a tough crowd, some with almost three decades of experience. The stringent questioning improves both the subject matter and presentation, helping prepare the project for the exigencies of the real world.

An important function of an urban designer is to integrate the requirements of numerous subsystems into the smooth operation of an overall system—a city. Each of those subsystems, including social networks, transportation, lighting, housing, shopping, landscape, way finding, and power (to name a very few), has its experts. Typically, these professionals are paid to calculate and produce drawings for finished systems, but for an urban designer, their input is much more valuable at the start of a project. Rather than make precise calculations, they should come together and make general estimates in the context of their co-professionals, looking for new synergies. For example, if a mechanical engineer is present with an architect and an urban designer to propose a street layout, the three can work together to set the streets to angle the buildings to minimize the solar gain and therefore reduce the need for mechanical systems. If a landscape specialist is present, perhaps they could decide how to angle a facade to serve as a green wall in summer, or to best retain storm water for irrigation.

Collegiality is an important way to balance outcomes. Professionals in individual disciplines are taught to maximize the particular variable they control. A traffic engineer might design for the

THE THREE PHASES OF URBAN DESIGN IN PRACTICE:
HARLEM CHILDREN'S ZONE

Geoffrey Canada is an educator whose goal is to end the cycle of poverty in Harlem. He has promised that every child in Harlem will go to college. Many know him as the subject of a movie on reforming education called *Waiting for Superman*. He runs an organization called the Harlem Children's Zone. To make good on his word, he combines public and private finance to build a series of charter schools, which he calls Promise Academies, to educate the children of Harlem who might otherwise drop out of the school system. He is an intense man and polite, but driven, impatient to reach his goals. When he needed to expand with another school for 1,300 children, he was worried that the urban design process would slow him down.

Geoffrey Canada weighs the options. *(Credit: Thaddeus Pawlowski)*

In November 2009, Canada had met with the head of the New York City Housing Authority (NYCHA), a public authority that owns acres of New York City land on which almost a half million people live in public housing. Most of this housing was built fifty years ago as part of the Robert Moses slum clearance program. Canada's idea was to bring a school right to the residents of public housing.

Our urban design group met Canada, and we were given a mission: to lead a planning effort with NYCHA and the Harlem Children's Zone and find a home for the new school in a way that would be as beneficial as possible for the community and the neighborhood.

Everyone involved had strong opinions. We had a deadline. We promised a consensus site plan by the first week in February 2010. We started out to design the question: what are we transforming and why? At first, Canada thought that asking such a broad question was wasting precious time we did not have, but by asking the question we quickly got a statement of goals out of each of the stakeholders. We did a quick urban design study on a public housing site, the St. Nicholas Houses, located on four New York City blocks that had been combined into a superblock in 1953; there are 1,417 units in thirteen towers. The superblock configuration had closed 129th Street in Harlem and isolated the housing from the surrounding community, and it had become a haven for gangs. The one bright spot was a grove of mature trees in the open center of the superblock.

If we designed a standard school for 1,300 kids, there would be only one place big enough to put it: right in the middle, on top of the forest of trees. Not only would the community lose its trees, but the school would be isolated within the housing, which was in turn isolated from the city around it. We needed to do better, but we didn't have much time.

We built a team of stakeholders, we established a design process with NYCHA, St. Nick's tenants' association, Harlem Children's Zone, and the school's builders, and we began meeting, first with the tenants' association, then with the school principals to lay out a program. We took site tours with Willie Mae Lewis, president of the tenants' association, to see how people used the space, and with NYCHA building management to see how the existing buildings operated. We met with the church groups on site, with merchants around the neighborhood, with other city agencies that would be in charge of approving every aspect of the development from storm water to traffic to construction to financing and educational standards.

At this point, we had a client in the many stakeholders who had to be kept happy. We had a site in that we would have to locate a sizable school somewhere in the housing development, and we had a program: a school within a community with before and after school programs that would go beyond K–12 to touch everyone from babies to retirees.

We had "designed the question" by articulating the clients' goals as design imperatives: for Harlem Children's Zone, to build a school on time and on budget with strong community integration; for NYCHA, to reopen the super-block with a city street, to minimize the building's footprint to preserve open space; and for City Planning, to support the goals of an area-wide rezoning and bring increased vibrancy and mixed uses to the neighborhood.

Now we had only a month to design the answer. Our promised product was a consensus site plan, which the school's architect would take over and use to design the school. We sketched with the team, built models, met again and again with the stakeholders. Every sketch would have political input; the project was now a top priority with City Hall. And every configuration of the school would have immediate financial impacts that would then reverberate to financial commitments already in place from the city and private-sector donation. The design kept changing as we tried to meet our stakeholders' goals. Finally the design was ready.

Now the urban design process entered the implementation phase. As urban designers, our role diminished to presentations and revisions. We held public meetings and kept everyone moving forward with visual communication. Of course there was dissent, some of it angry. Nothing happens easily in cities. People who oppose charter schools in general attacked the project in specific for its street, for its bulk, for its cost, trying to kill the school before it could be born. There was screaming at hearings, but the voices of parents and students desperate for a chance

at a good school in their neighborhood eventually overcame the entrenched interests. Approvals in hand, the only thing remaining was to fill a budget gap. The city could give no more, so Canada reached out to his board and to the private sector. In a matter of weeks, he had raised millions from Google, Goldman Sachs, and some of the city's wealthiest philanthropists. The project was a go.

We opened 129th Street to connect the project to the city's street grid and lined it with new trees and benches. We put the new school's building height along the new street, bringing a thousand new "eyes on the street" that would eliminate the gangs' influence over public space. And we preserved most of the central stand of trees, landscaping the area as an amenity to the residents and a backdrop for the school.

At the groundbreaking we felt a sense of success. The plan was a result of an urban design process. We were not on the podium, we were not called out by name, but the shovels were transforming the city to accomplish our goals, the ones we distilled from our clients, the stakeholders. The simple urban design act of putting a city street back into the superblock of the public housing project was a statement that the isolation of public housing was a thing of the past. Placing a school on that street reconnected the children to the opportunity around them. Construction was on schedule, and Canada was satisfied with the process of urban design.

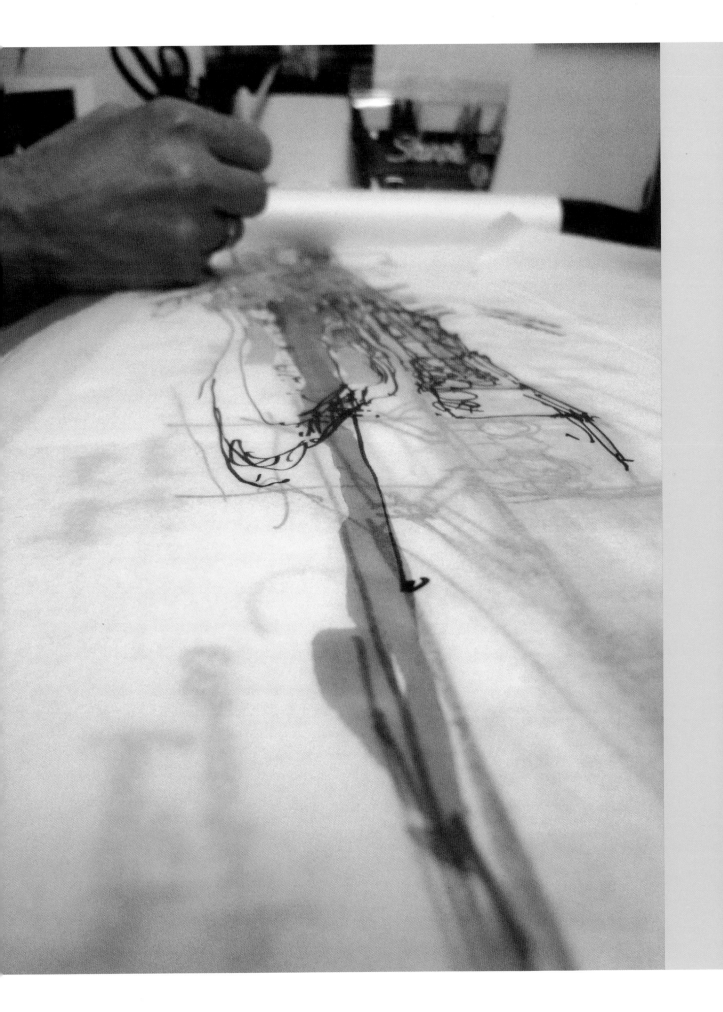

Collegiality.

(Credit: Alexandros Washburn)

maximum flow of cars in the least amount of time; a mechanical engineer might seek to maintain the steadiest temperature with the least air flow. Collegiality can bring those professionals together and let them see that maximizing their variable might degrade the quality and performance of the overall system. A traffic solution that improves the flow of cars by 10 percent might impede the flow of pedestrians by 100 percent. I have seen some engineers eliminate pedestrian crossings entirely to make it marginally easier for a car to turn a corner. If they understand that improving pedestrian flow is part of their job and that balance of the system as a whole is the goal, engineers—as design professionals—can help find a solution.

Collegial design techniques, whether involving the public, peers, or interdisciplinary groups, are a way of increasing urban design's intelligence far above the insight of a single person. The urban designer should use the collegial process as a way to develop shared values so that the best thinking can come to the design. It is never an embarrassment for an urban designer not to know the answer; it is a failing only not to ask.

The implementation phase of the urban design cycle is in essence a series of tests applied to an urban design hypothesis, or vision. The tests come from the community, the markets, the government, or other designers. If there is a fit among the politics, finance, and design, the project passes the test; if not, back to the drawing board. Not surprisingly, the urban designers are often playing catch-up to changes being made for political and financial reasons. In designing a master plan for the redevelopment of Coney Island, we had to constantly revise drawings to reflect the shifting negotiations between a landowner and the city. Every deal point resulted in a new site, a new program; the urban design had to be revised to fit, otherwise there would have been no hope of implementation.

Urban design's goal is transformation, to build a bridge from the status quo to the future.

Any product of urban design requires testing in order to be implemented. The testing consists of "what if" scenarios as simple as sketches or as complex as environmental impact statements based on the proposed rule, plan, or project. The key to understanding testing in urban design is the uncertainty surrounding the concept of transformation. The transformation intended by the products of urban design may take decades to unfold and may be irreversible. It is critical to test the intended effect of those products before they are implemented.

Testing takes many forms. The simplest is the "prevent the worst, permit the best" analysis we employ when considering a new urban design rule. The tower-top rule adopted for the rezoning of the Hudson rail yards is an example. We had rezoned the area for eight major new skyscrapers, some taller than the Empire State Building. These new buildings would have a major impact on the skyline of Manhattan. We wanted to prevent the worst, which in the case of the tower tops would have been identical flat roofs with air conditioners on top. We also wanted to permit the best, such as the most expressive shapes being built in the world today. We tested our rule on hundreds of tower tops before presenting it to the planning commission. It passed the test, and is now law. However, it may take decades to fully build out the yards and to test our rule in the real world.

There are many more technical forms of testing in the urban design process, ranging from real estate pro forma analysis to environmental impact statements. In an era of growth during climate change, I believe the most important measures of testing will involve determining whether an urban design product has a measurable, significant impact on sustainability. In chapter 5, we will discuss further the need for a system of ecometrics to gauge our progress toward sustainability and to guide our urban design process toward achieving it.

Implementation has different end points for the different products of urban design. If the urban design product is a rule, implementation means enactment and enforcement. If the product is a plan, then implementation means adoption. If the product is a pilot project, then implementation means construction. Implementation is rarely in the hands of the urban designer if he or she is acting as a designer. Rather, implementation in the urban design process relies on the forces of politics and finance. You can draw a plan in isolation, but to get it followed you need political power and financial resources.

As an urban designer, you believe that what you draw affects the quality of life of your fellow citizens. You are passionate and believe that design can provide new solutions to avert the catastrophe of global warming with plans for cities that are carbon neutral and energy positive. So it is a disappointment to realize how little chance of implementation your ideas have without the support of politics and finance. No matter how good the idea, if the political will is absent, or if the money is insufficient, it will not be implemented.

The hurdles for implementation differ for each product of urban design. A plan requires some political cajoling for adoption, but in the end, it is just a plan. No one needs to stick to it. However, a rule requires a much bigger political lift. If implemented, it wins the legal power of enforcement and gains the weight of the governing organization behind it. Rules, such as a limitation on how much or how high you can build, are not passed easily. Each rule affects somebody's money, and as the saying goes, don't get between a man and his lunch. Implementing a rule means figuring out how to keep those with a vote happy. The transfer of development rights in the West Chelsea rezoning was a masterful example of using an urban design rule to keep financial interests happy and garner political approval to build something that greatly improves civic life. But to implement an actual pilot project, to actually build the High Line park, rather than just to enact its supporting rules, is entirely another level of achievement. To implement a rule, you need to align the politics, finance, and design only for the moment of voting it into law. To implement a project, you have to keep those three aligned for as long as it takes to build, which can be decades. That is why truly transformative projects—urban design projects—are so rare. Aligning politics, finance, and design sounds like an exercise in Euclidian geometry, but it is more like stuffing three cats into a bag. They want to get out.

Politics

The decision-making process of politics, through the actions of government, affects urban design at every scale from national tax policy to local building permits. The degree to which this effect is overt varies from country to country. Singapore makes urban development a top national priority and uses every means of communication to articulate the policy. The U.S. federal government pretends a laissez-faire approach to planning. There is no overt national development policy, only a series of seemingly disconnected programs, as disparate as funding for clean

An urban designer must understand finance and politics as well
as design.
(Credit: Alexandros Washburn)

coal, low gasoline taxes, and home mortgage interest deductibility, that in the aggregate have favored suburbanization. Some call the net effect of the various programs a "hidden" policy.

In the United States, urban design implementation faces the problem that regions are not empowered politically. New York, New Jersey, and Connecticut are three states that form a region, yet they have no level of common governance. There is federal governance and state governance, but no entity with the power to tax and act in the public benefit operates across all three. Therefore, regional decisions such as watershed management and rail transportation are left to the goodwill of the participants—not a recipe for success in politics.

As you go down from the level of city to the neighborhood, the politics becomes more and more personal. The people screaming at the Harlem Children's Zone hearings were neighbors (see Box 2.1). The emotions were real, understandably so—the project will change lives and affect livelihoods. It is

difficult to stand in a room and be yelled at, but an urban designer might as well get used to it. It is our job to "take a few tomatoes," as my boss, Amanda Burden, says. Sometimes, taking those tomatoes is the first messy step in gaining understanding and reaching agreement.

From federal policy to regional programs to local approvals, the process of urban design implementation requires political agreement at every step. Byzantine or straightforward, fashioning a project that can get that agreement while still improving the lives of its citizens is part of the urban designer's job that has very little to do with design. It is politics, pure and simple.

Finance

Implementation also requires that the urban design project have its finances in order. Just passing muster with the forces of politics is not enough; the project must make sense to the markets or have a subsidy that came along with its political approval. The subsidy can take the form of mandates or incentives, sticks or carrots, but rarely is government money alone enough to complete a transformation of a neighborhood. However, the object of the urban design process is not to complete a transformation but to start it; relatively little funding may be required at the start.

The essential calculation for urban designers is the time value of money. What is the value today of a stream of rents in the future? This depends on the "hurdle rate"—what your money could be getting elsewhere at similar levels of risk, assumptions of inflation, and a few other subtleties. In terms of urban design, it is a way of deciding whether constructing a building is a good investment.

In finance, risk and reward are linked. A high return might be an indication of high underlying risk. Buying stocks can be speculative, even bonds can be deemed junk. People can miscalculate a market and buildings can stand empty. There is no end of risk in finance, and we are always mispricing risk and going through boom and bust cycles.

But buildings have an enduring appeal, and when the numbers work, the buildings multiply, and the cities grow by repetition. When we overbuild, the market corrects, or as in the recent Great Recession, governments around the world organize a bailout.

I dwell on the subject of risk because it is not well enough understood in the process of urban design. As we will see in chapter 5, risk is at the center of the sustainability question, and urban designers are inadvertently increasing climate change risk to cities if they do not understand the relation between probability and consequences. As Tom Friedman, of the *New York Times*, likes to say, "Nature doesn't do bailouts." Any climate change risk we incur in seeking higher real estate returns had better be accounted for because it won't be forgiven.

In seeking those higher returns, we often cut corners in building our cities. A highway is cheaper than a subway. A less efficient heating system costs less to buy but uses more energy in operation. A wall with less insulation is cheaper than a wall with more.

These financial decisions all increase greenhouse gas emissions. We ignore such emissions when we calculate our returns; in technical terms, we treat them as *externalities* outside our financial equations.

Treating such costs as externalities boosts our rate of return, but it hides our higher risk profile. This should be a warning because a higher return with an even higher risk is no bargain. We need to move to cost-benefit analyses whose inputs are as broad as possible in our framework for decision making on larger projects. If successful, a system of sustainable financial implementation for urban design would reward and multiply those actions that have a significant positive impact on the environment, on the economy, and ultimately on society. We have far to go in developing such a system, so for the present, urban design implementation is left to the traditional equations of profit and loss.

Design

This book in its entirety is a treatise on design, but in comparing design to politics and finance, the lessons are clear. Of the three forces of politics, finance, and design that must align for the transformation of cities, design is always the weakest. So an urban designer must make hay while the sun shines. Take advantage of the alignment of the larger forces to accomplish what you aim, but recognize when the circumstances have changed. Charles McKim, who literally moved mountains through urban design to transform the National Mall in Washington, D.C., a century ago, failed to recognize that his design mandate expired when his political benefactor died. A few years after the adoption of his plans, he wasted what remained of his health and political capital fighting a cocky new secretary of agriculture determined to place his headquarters a few feet over McKim's regulating line on the Mall. McKim died beaten and shunned, having forgotten to follow his own dictum, "you can compromise everything but the essence." The essence of the National Mall has been revealed over time, the Department of Agriculture building has faded into the background, and the space has become what Kim originally intended: the greatest gathering place in America.

Anyone versed in politics, finance, and design can become an urban designer, but what happens when one person reaches the pinnacle of all three overlapping fields at once? He or she can transform the city with stunning breadth and speed. One such person is Brazilian Jaime Lerner, former mayor of Curitiba, Brazil. Politician, financier, designer, top-down executive, and bottom-up activist, in one life he lived all the lives of those who can shape a city. He brilliantly and rapidly changed the status quo to transform his native Curitiba into one of the most livable, sustainable, and fast-growing cities in South America. For doing so, I consider him among the world's greatest living urban designers. He graduated with a degree in architecture and urban planning in 1965. He was in power as mayor of Curitiba for three separate terms between 1971 and 1992. When he was mayor, he believed he had a responsibility to be the city's chief design officer. He used extremely creative means to build a network of parks, to extend municipal services to the barrios, to knit the city together with bus rapid transit. There are few people who can change a city fast enough to see their own legacy built and validate their vision in the thriving daily life of its citizens. Jaime Lerner is one of them. But political power is fleeting, and his urban design accomplishments come with a hint of nostalgia. No longer a mayor, now a consultant, he likes to joke, "I used to be my own best client."

VALUES IN URBAN DESIGN

We said that the process of urban design was complex, iterative, and nested. If you have been through it a few times, you might rather say it is maddening, unending, and irrational. Not an ideal process, perhaps, yet one that has been stubbornly consistent since before the time of the ancient Athenians and, I believe, one that will remain in place far into the future because it is human nature to fight for what we care about, and we care about our cities.

I would like to conclude this chapter with a step back from the foibles of process and instead consider the values that underlie it; the point of view that guides an urban designer through the process.

How do you make everyday choices in the urban design process? For instance, would it be better to plan for a school, a factory, or a waterfront park? What if the factory emitted huge amounts of carbon, but gave a community good jobs? These are the sorts of choices that are embedded in a program. They are difficult choices to make, and it is not the urban designer's role to make them unilaterally, but rather to help visualize them and account for their consequences in the bigger picture and let the client and community make the choice.

The biggest picture challenge today is climate change, and meeting that challenge has to be first on the agenda of any urban design solution. But it is important to remember that the goal of cities in fighting climate change is to achieve sustainability. To be sustainable, a city needs to be attractive; to be attractive, it must provide good jobs. It wouldn't matter that a city emitted no carbon if it had no jobs, because sooner or later, it would have no citizens. Social cohesion is necessary for sustainability as well. A city with no justice would be little better than a city with no jobs. It would be a work camp, not a city, and would not be sustainable in competition with cities that people enjoyed living in.

The process of urban design can not solve these complex social, economic, and environmental problems. But the process of urban design can help a community visualize a desired future in which social, economic, and environmental needs are balanced and met. It can help guide the transformation, and most importantly, it can articulate the civic virtues such as prudence, thrift, and creativity that are needed to sustain the transformation.

If we do not adapt our cities to the effects of climate change, mitigate our carbon emissions, and substitute renewable resources for those we are depleting, then we will destroy our urban way of life, no matter how much justice, riches, or beauty we have put into our cities. First and foremost, the urban design process should be directed toward climate change—the environment in triple bottom line accounting. If there is to be a factory, then let's be creative to mitigate its carbon and make it sustainable.

And what of social justice? In its world development report of 2009, the World Bank noted that concentrating economic density and diversity in cities leads to economic development. However, economic development also leads to increases in social disparities. The conclusion the World Bank comes to is that cities must address these imbalances as part of their growth strategy, not least by reducing the poorer population's higher exposure to threats of climate change by adapting the city to protect them.

So when triple bottom line accounting is applied to urban design, the environment comes first; not as an end in itself, but as a means of achieving the social and economic goals that make a city sustainable. The ultimate purpose of urban design is the improvement of civic life. Each generation of urban designers must judge what is the greatest challenge to civic life and make sure that the process of urban design addresses it first.

To advance a set of values through the complexity of the urban design process requires establishing a consistent point of view. "Point of view" is more than a figure of speech in urban design. Because the urban design process is essentially one of visualization, a point of view is necessary to represent an idea visually; the point of view enables others to see what the urban designer is seeing.

Different points of view are adapted to different value systems. A bird's-eye point of view works well for systems that promote order over experience. A driver's point of view works well when the chief value of a society is the promotion of personal mobility. From a driver's point of view, clues of scale and convenience once sized to the human body warp with the speed and distance of automobile travel. For the driver, the spatial needs for sight lines, turning radii, and parking spaces dominate design decisions for shaping the public realm.

Points of view are often in conflict, as are the value systems they represent. The driver's perspective is often at odds with the pedestrian's perspective. If a road swells to eight lanes to move cars, it becomes hopeless for a pedestrian to cross. The urban designer must ask: what is more important, to move cars or to move people?

I believe in the primacy of the pedestrian point of view. I believe that values that respect the environment, the economy, and society are best represented by a point of view that is sustainable, humanist, and experiential—the pedestrian point of view is all of these. This pedestrian point of view is humanist because it puts every decision at a human eye level. Because the street is public and experienced by all citizens, the perspective presupposes a concern for social equity; everyone has a right to the benefit of public space. Because the pedestrian comes first, the perspective is sustainable. The perspective

I believe in the primacy of the pedestrian point of view.

highlights the great carbon savings of walkability, giving us our first best hope in helping our cities combat climate change. This leads me to believe that the best point of view for urban design in the era of growth during climate change is the pedestrian point of view.

Taking the pedestrian point of view is not simplistic; it also allows quantification of both small- and large-scale decisions. By applying the pedestrian perspective, the urban designer can judge everything from street furniture to infrastructure. The perspective allows door-to-door trip comparison on whether it is faster, cheaper, and more sustainable to "walk" between cities by hopping on transit to catch a train rather than flying or driving. Enormous numbers of highly complex infrastructural decisions can be made in support of system efficiency by consistently applying the pedestrian's perspective.

Finally, coming from New York, it seems odd to me that the dictionary definition of "pedestrian" means "ordinary." On New York's streets, pedestrian means "fabulous." Stars from Sinatra to Jay-Z have written songs about New York's streets. There are few experiences in the world as exhilarating as walking down the street in New York on a summer evening. This applies to world-famous districts as well as to out-of-the-way neighborhoods. I have felt this exhilaration on Fifth Avenue at Rockefeller Center, and also on 37th Avenue in Jackson Heights, Queens. To be a part of the density, the diversity, and the democracy of the multitude of people pulsing through a public space is glorious. I love New York City streets, and my values are to make them better and better with every urban design action I take.

The expression of values in the urban design process requires the application of judgment. Judgment requires a consistent point of view. No matter how maddening, unending, or irrational I might feel the urban design process to be at any given moment, I can get through it with the right values and point of view. My point of view is that of the pedestrian, and my values are to bring a measure of prudence, thrift, and creativity to the growth of my city and the improvement of its civic life. But in the urban design process, *my* values matter little. It is the ability to let a community see through a common point of view and to act upon shared values that changes first the city and then, perhaps, the world.

Pedestrian is judge.

(Credit: Skye Duncan)

Drawing and redrawing. *(Credit: Alexandros Washburn)*

Opposite page: Modeling the city of Singapore.
(Credit: Lay Bee Yap)

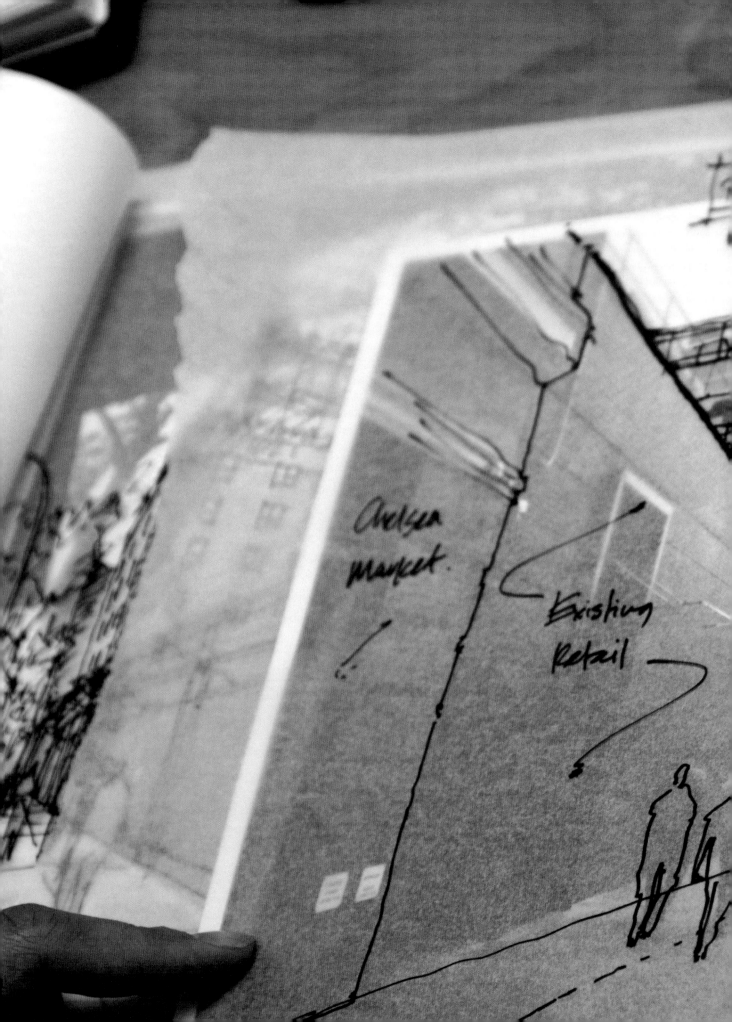

The hand of Jeff Shumaker at work on Manhattan. *(Credit: Alexandros Washburn)*

Houses.

+ New Residential.

top (2 stories)

The city is never finished.
View of Hong Kong.
(Credit: Alexandros Washburn)

Paley Park on 52nd Street in midtown
Manhattan is tiny, almost hidden, but
its waterfall and grove of honey locust
trees instantly calms you. My daughter
Lelia was mesmerized.
(Credit: Alexandros Washburn)

CHAPTER 3

THE PRODUCTS OF URBAN DESIGN

The products of urban design act as game changers that lay down new ways for the city to grow. It is a misconception that urban designers make cities. They don't; instead they make products—rules, plans, and projects—that guide a city's transformation.

The process of urban design may feel never ending, but the products are discreet, actionable, and designed to change the status quo. For instance, as we saw in the last chapter, in every phase of its realization, the Harlem Children's Zone used the products of urban design to succeed. These products were rules, such as changes to the zoning code; plans, such as the consensus master plan for the St. Nicholas housing site; and the built project itself, the new school and the new street, which physically transformed the areas that surround them.

Urban design operates at all scales except that of the city itself. Remember, urban design makes the tools that build cities; urban design does not build the city itself. To say that the city itself is an urban design project is a dangerous tautology that leads the urban designer either to a stultifying sameness in design of new cities or to an inability to get beyond process in the case of existing cities.

Everything is connected to everything in urban design, and no one designer can pretend to encompass the totality. Instead, an urban designer must acknowledge that a healthy city is never finished and recognize that the products of urban design are specific links in a chain of urban transformation that will go on long after he or she has departed.

The process of urban design was outlined in chapter 2, making a distinction between transformation and repetition in the growth of cities. Transformation refers to the relatively rare moments when political, financial, and design consensus is reached to change the rules of the game and establish a new status quo, whether for a small district or the entire city. Repetition refers to the process of building, over and over, in a manner that does not require further change to the rules, only compliance with the status quo. In New York, we call this sort of building "as of right." If you follow the existing zoning code and building codes, you are entitled to build and no one has the right to stop you or force you to change your designs. Projects that happen as of right are not urban design, though their designers need to understand the intent of urban design to properly interpret and comply with the rules.

...even the regulation of buildings can determine the character of the public space between them.

Those rules have varied historically. At one extreme is the baroque city, laid out by a central authority with elaborate street plans accompanied by very strict guidelines for the building out of individual parts to achieve a calculated effect over time. Washington, D.C., is such a city, and its vast radial avenues are still filling out two centuries after its initial planning.

The other extreme is the fractal city. In a fractal city, there is less overt order, and it may appear more chaotic. New York is a fractal city; the building

out of each parcel occurs at different times under different rules and financial and technical conditions, producing the irregular skyscraper forest of Manhattan. Each project changes the balance, like a bird setting down on a wire, and affects the next project; urban design must be taken into consideration at each step. As a result, the transformative effect of urban design can be felt simultaneously at multiple scales, from an individual parcel to the infrastructure grid of the entire city. The suppleness of a fractal city, its ability to change, puts great emphasis on urban design to examine and discover the underlying order of the status quo, to reinterpret it, and to propose change that will realign the rules with the city's contemporary goals. If you compare zoning maps of New York over time, you can see the increasingly fine grain of the pattern.[1] The zoning code is a living document, able to change and adapt over time.

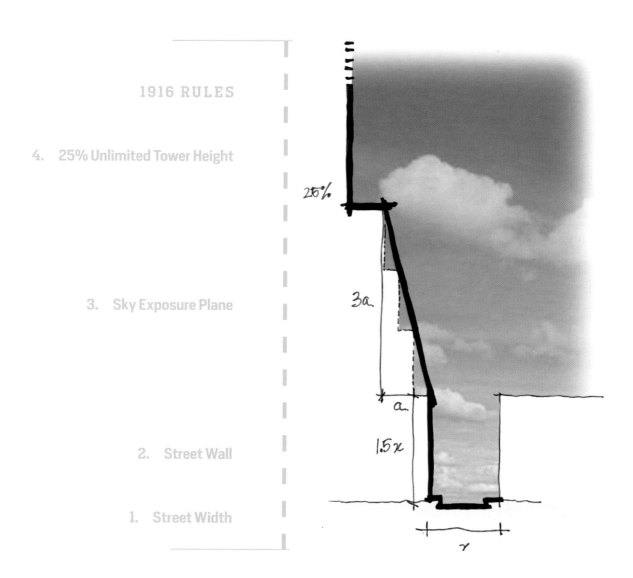

URBAN DESIGN PRODUCTS: RULES

Urban design rules vary by scale and specificity. Urban policy is the largest and least specific form of rule. Building codes are the most specific. The rules most commonly associated with urban design—zoning rules—operate at the city and neighborhood scales. Every scale of urban design rules can change the public character of the city; even the regulation of buildings can determine the character of the public space between them.

Policy

Policy is a set of political directions set at the highest levels of government that provide the outline for more specific programs at smaller scales of government. If a government has a fiscal policy, for instance, it will serve to align actions by its executive departments and coordinate the thousands of lines of tax code so that specific governmental actions on borrowing, spending, and taxation are not counter to the general governmental intent of the policy.

To survive politically, policies must prove popular. In a democracy, that usually means there has to be something for everyone—or at least the majority. Before 2007, less than half the people on Earth lived in cities. Now that has changed and urbanites are the majority. Maybe there is hope that urban design will now be considered more openly as policy all across the urbanizing world. If that policy aims to make cities sustainable, individual programs of the status quo can be judged, confronted, and ceased if found contrary to the purposes of the urban design policy.

Urban policy at the federal level is the largest scale of urban design rules applied to guide the growth and form of cities to help meet national objectives. The Netherlands has a federal urban policy to coordinate the growth of its four largest cities into a region, the Randstad, and integrate their built form with a green heart of open space and open water. The United States is uncomfortable with the notion of federal urban policy. A legacy of the poverty that tore apart its cities in the last generation, urban policy here is seen by many as a code word for welfare. When a southern congressman labeled New York City "a black hole of waste," he was playing to the suburban voting base of his home district. In reality, New York City is no black hole; it generates billions of dollars more in revenue for the federal government than it receives back in aid, which was the reverse of the congressman's district. I mention this political mudslinging in the context of urban design because it is about time that we acknowledge the vital role cities in the United States play in the health of the nation's economy. An urban designer has to know the fiscal facts. Cities make money, nations spend it. The design of cities offers the nation many solutions to a variety of its challenges, from economic development to energy and land conservation. Those advantages can only develop on a national scale if federal urban policy supports urban design.

Every country has a fiscal policy, but very few countries have an urban design policy. Singapore, because of its limited supply of land and great demand upon it, had no choice but to consciously ponder, choose, and implement a series of urban design strategies to transform the city-state from jungle to metropolis. Each policy cycle had as its object the transformation of the island into an increasingly dense urbanized area; the current policy cycle includes increasing the amount of permeable and planted area to increase the resilience of the island to drought, flood, and heat. The central government used the policy to coordinate all the tools at its disposal to accomplish this, updating its master plan every five years to reflect progress.

An urban designer has to know the fiscal facts. Cities make money, nations spend it.

Policy need not be stated to cause great transformations in the design of cities. During the era of the interstate highway, the United States had no official urban design policy, letting the issue of urban form fall to the free market. Behind this equanimity was a "hidden" policy of government to actively promote the growth of suburbia. The hidden policy worked by purposing seemingly unrelated programs to the same end. Thus federal home mortgage subsidies for World War II veterans, when combined with federal financing of the new interstate highways, effectively formed a policy of suburbanization.

Urban policy is a powerful subject that has engaged great minds throughout history. It is also a subject for a limited number of urban designers. Those with an aptitude for visualizing the coordinated effect of government programs and a stomach for the process of legislation and the mudslinging that accompanies it will find that policy can engineer some of the greatest transformations yet to be imagined in cities.

The Basics of Rules

If you have the authority to enforce it, the simplest urban design product is a rule, often called a code, such as a building code. One example of an ancient urban design rule is, "No street shall be narrower than the width of a laden donkey." Applied to an entire city, this rule benefits the entire populace, ensuring that no part of the city is impassable. It transforms the status quo ante, when too-close houses may have choked commerce and communication, isolating certain neighborhoods in the community. It's a good rule, and it's still in force today on the island of Hydra in Greece.

Rules have multiplied in the modern world, and many of these rules have gone global. The New York City Building Code is now based on the International Building Code. Energy codes are being compared across countries and an international standard of energy efficiency is conceivable. But the interpretation of codes remains stubbornly local.

The process of modern rulemaking can be traced back to the Act for Rebuilding London of 1667, which was created in response to the Great Fire of London in 1666. The Act for Rebuilding mandated brick and stone construction, minimum street widths, a forty-foot no-build strip along the Thames to provide ready access to firefighting water, and a table of building types and corresponding thicknesses to the fireproof party walls between them.

Rulemaking increased in complexity in the nineteenth century when it became clear that the spread of infectious disease could be prevented through changes in the built environment. The regulations were the only way to safely accommodate the unprecedented densities of urban populations before the invention of mass transit would allow those populations to spread out. At its peak, the Lower East Side of Manhattan was considered to be the densest major settlement in history; the densest block housed 2,200 people crowded into the cheapest sort of buildings. Reformers pushed for the passage of the first Tenement House Act in 1867 as a rule to mandate a toilet and sewer connection in each of the buildings.

Plumbing codes, health codes, and residential building codes joined the fire codes in an effort to ensure a minimum of light, air, water, and sewer services to citizens in the nineteenth century. The nineteenth-century health-based codes saved the city from the life-threatening perils of its own density. How to shape that density became the subject of the next century's set of rules: zoning.

ZONING

Zoning is a system of building regulation applied to a map of the city to achieve a desired pattern of density and land use. Originally theorized in the 1870s by Professor Reinhard Baumeister of Karlsruhe, the zoning system was successfully applied to the large German city of Frankfurt in 1891. The zoning system worked by classifying buildings according to use, such as residence, factory, and mixed-use, as well as according to density, with factors for heights, lot coverage, and sun angles. The basic principle was that the innermost zone of the city would be the densest, with building cornice heights greater than the width of the street, and blocks built solid with only internal courts to provide light and air in interior rooms. All uses were

Looking up at the Equitable
Building, Manhattan. *(Credit:
Alexandros Washburn)*

allowed. In the next zones, density decreased: the height of buildings allowed became lower, and the portion of the lot required to be left open increased. The zones are then divided by use. A "country zone" with the least density of all encircled the city.

The high degree of control that this system allowed German building officials led to both a high degree of complexity as well as an ability to precisely control the resulting architecture with a mixture of tact and compulsion in the process of awarding building permits.

The regulatory complexity and all-powerful bureaucracy of the German system would seem anathema to the free-market spirit of America, particularly to the financers of Wall Street in the early twentieth century. So it is a great irony of urban design that Wall Street was the catalyst for the regulation that brought a form of German zoning to America.

You could say the issue began with a crime—the theft of light and air. When the Equitable Insurance Company put up a 538-foot tall building in the financial district intended to maximize the use of their valuable plot of real estate, they allowed for no setback. They built straight up from the lot lines. The boxy building stood as a proud monument to unfettered capitalism until the capitalists who owned the lots next door realized that they had been beggared. They realized too late that the Equitable Building took all their light and air and rendered their adjoining plots less valuable.

In February 1913, the mayor formed a committee of New York's top business and political leaders in response, which produced the "Report of the Heights of Buildings Commission" nine months later. The report laid out a plan to map zoning districts all across New York where the height and shape of buildings would be controlled. This report became the basis for the 1916 New York Zoning Law, which codified the

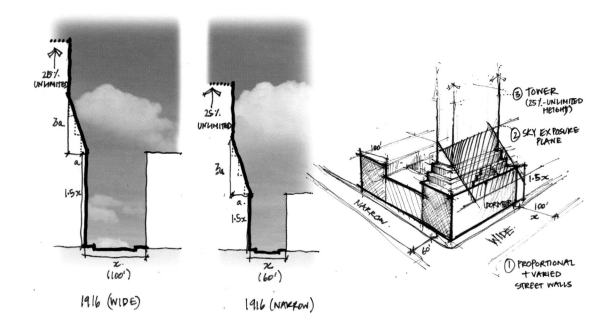

1916 (WIDE)

1916 (NARROW)

③ TOWER (25%-UNLIMITED HEIGHT)

② SKY EXPOSURE PLANE

① PROPORTIONAL + VARIED STREET WALLS

The regulations and zoning of New York City have shaped not only the city but the buildings, sometimes with amazing results, as in the Chrysler Building. [Credits [right] Skye Duncan, [left] Photo © David Pedre. Courtesy of iStockphoto.]

findings. The law changed the status quo of building in New York to ensure that light and air reached the street and no building occluded it neighbors. The urban design rule precluded boxy towers; instead, buildings competed for the tallest and most remarkable pyramidal form. The law stood the tests of the courts and the markets, and it guided the complete transformation of New York with masterworks such as the Chrysler Building. The rule is set out on page 109 in the section on form-based codes, but 1916 zoning achieved some pretty good urban design results for a relatively simple rule!

Those rules formed a status quo for almost fifty years. They were finally restructured by the 1961 zoning resolution, an urban design revolution that got rid of the earlier zoning's setback requirements. These had made it difficult to build cheaply the large, repetitive floors of office space piled high that developers wished to erect in the booming city.

Yet the public argument against the old zoning was that it provided too much space and the city would grow too large. The argument went that if the developers completely built out the permitted building envelope on every block from the 1916 zoning, the city would consist of a set of buildings large enough to house a population of 53 million people. To limit and direct growth, 1961 zoning introduced a new concept, floor-area ratio, in which each plot of land was assigned a maximum amount of space that could be built upon it, giving city experts lot-by-lot control of density. Allowable use groups were invented with zealous specificity and mapped to every plot.

New bulk regulations were invented for scores of new zoning districts. The new zoning resolution was an expert's dream: a place for everything and everything in its place in what was then the largest city in the world. It was a triumph for the city envisioned by Robert Moses. The 1961 zoning code officially adapted the city to the automobile and made Moses's favorite "tower in the park" housing schemes as of right.

Those schemes are not my favorite, and I actively dislike the "height factor" building envelope rules embedded in the 1961 amendment that continue to permit them. But I am a believer in the process of amendment to the zoning code that the 1961 rules embody, and which we have developed over time into a living document. New York City does not have a master plan. Instead, the city uses the combination of its zoning text and zoning map amendments to record our aspirations for the city's growth. We have codified the process of their revision (the top-down, bottom-up conga dance of the Uniform Land Use Review Procedure, discussed in chapter 2), and the result is a continuously evolving, constantly adapting document of increasing specificity to guide the city's growth. In the past decade alone, we have rezoned more than one-third of the city.

We will rely on zoning to make the city more sustainable and more resilient. We have already enacted Zone Green, a series of zoning changes to encourage more sustainable building and the reduction of carbon emissions. One critical change is to identify and remove old portions of the code that inadvertently prevented sustainable practices. For instance, solar panels didn't exist as domestic devices in 1961 and were never included in the definition of "permitted obstructions" that could be placed on roofs. That has now been changed. After Hurricane Sandy, the zoning code will be tested as a tool to encourage flood-proof buildings or otherwise make the city more resilient

to flooding. Will the zoning code be able to catalyze these changes? This is a question being answered in real time by New York and cities across the globe, and it will test the effectiveness of zoning as a system of rules for transformation.

The legal representation of the zoning system, text and maps, is in for an overhaul. Words and lines seem inadequate in a world where computer modeling is powerful enough to represent an entire city in three dimensions. Every floor of every building, existing or proposed, every bulk envelope of every block is or will soon be available for viewing and consideration by anyone through the Internet. The ability to propose and preview alternative futures and then memorialize specific approvals in law is tantalizing. Already there are apps for cell phones and tablets that let you point your device at an existing space and an image of a proposed change is superimposed on the picture. This is called augmented reality, and could be combined with cloud-sourced input to effectively "vote" on the desirability of a change. The control afforded by these new technologies seems immense and novel. Yet it is probably no more powerful than the discretion afforded to the early German bürgermeisters, who used the power of the first zoning laws, vague as they were, to achieve the most precise results. Ultimately, it is not the power itself but how we use it that determines the form of the city. We should use that power sparingly. Urban designers must remember that it is not their role to design everything; it is their role to analyze the rules of the status quo and to transform those rules so that others will then fill in the design with variety and fresh vigor.

The increasingly fine grain of New York City zoning and land use maps (a) 1916, (b) 1961, (c) 2013. *(Credit: New York City Department of City Planning)*

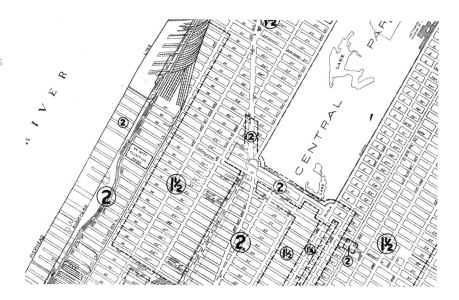

Zoning is an evolving tool of urban design, and I see three general directions that are changing the way that planning is carried out. In each, the end result is more specificity.

• **Form-based zoning** is a tool designed to replace traditional zoning, which is based on land use regulation, with a system based on regulating building form. Typically, a form-based system will include a regulating plan designating where different building forms apply; building form standards regulating permitted configuration and features of buildings, particularly in relation to the public realm; and public-space standards, regulating the design of streets and plazas. The 1916 New York City zoning code was the original form-based code and any new form-based code would do well to study its simplicity and restraint.

Form-based zoning works best when stripped to its essentials, such as the original 1916 New York City zoning code, which I consider (and here I am, of course, completely without bias) the best form-based code ever written. It's simple: you take the width of your street and multiply it. This gives you your base height. From there, a regulating line angles back from the street. When that line reaches twenty-five percent of your lot, the sky's the limit.

The form-based code system will include administrative procedures and definitions of all legally binding terms. What the system does not include are many of the techniques first showcased in the

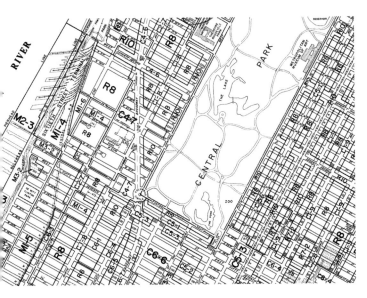

1961 New York City zoning amendment: floor-area ratios, open-space ratios, and any other algorithmic bulk controls. Form-based zoning also does not limit land use by district, and typically encourages mixed-use configurations.

Form-based zoning is identified with the New Urbanist movement and often carries with it the neotraditional aesthetic of building forms so strongly advocated by this group. To the degree that those aesthetic standards are prescriptive, the movement loses applicability to the

rapidly changing cities of the world. Traditional buildings contain important lessons embedded in their details and ornament, particularly with respect to how a building makes a street. We should certainly study them and respect their lessons. But new materials such as glass embedded with light-emitting diodes constantly challenge the tectonics of the old aesthetic. New demands for resource production in buildings, from the integration of solar cells to rooftop farming, require new shapes to carry them.

Grand Central Station was given landmark status in 1978. *(Credit: Alex Proimos. Accessed through Wikimedia Commons.)*

- **Protected historic districts or landmarks** have affected zoning by ensuring that new construction is in keeping with the character of existing historic buildings or districts. These are called contextual districts and are designed to maintain the overall form and massing of the neighboring buildings while providing adequate floor plates for modern uses.

The historic preservation movement was catalyzed in 1964 by the demolition of New York's great Pennsylvania Station, considered one of America's finest works of architecture. The historic preservation law was passed in 1965 with the goal of preserving the historic fabric of New York City. The law saved New York's other great station, Grand Central Terminal, from demolition by permitting the transfer of the building rights of the land on which it sits (its air rights) to adjacent building sites. The legality of the transfer principle was upheld by the courts, and it became common practice to protect buildings and then entire districts with landmark status.

I believe in historic preservation as a tool of challenging the present to surpass the past. If a building is deemed historic and left standing when a new building is built next to it, the new building can be compared in every detail with the old. Particularly from the pedestrian point of view, it can set a very high standard.

- **Algorithmic zoning** is a new development that harnesses computers to accelerate an iterative urban design process. Algorithmic zoning starts with a mathematical model of any traditional zoning rule, such as floor-area ratio. Based on a set of starting data for the equations, it generates different possible solutions for a study area, for instance, building envelopes for a certain amount of program square footage on a particular set of building lots. The algorithm then applies a second-order sorting principle to choose among the possible solutions and iterates the calculation for the next site. The algorithm can include randomization functions that induce variety, or it can expand the second-order sorting characteristics to include social or economic inputs. After a number of iterations, it has generated a model of what a particular area might become over time given a certain set of zoning rules and external forces.

The promise of algorithmic zoning is that it can help analyze complexity in the interaction of otherwise simple zoning rules over time, allowing the urban designer to look forward without over specifying results. The result could be the development of a system of zoning that is prescriptive enough to ensure fine-grain results while being general enough to accommodate dynamic growth. In some ways, the constant revision of New York City's existing zoning resolution through the process of rezoning and rebuilding is a slow-motion form of algorithmic design, in which project by project the city constantly changes the relation of one building to the next under an applied set of rules. As a new generation of designers becomes familiar with commonly available software that now exists for algorithmic design, a practical application of automated algorithmic zoning may not be far off.

Guidelines

Where zoning ends, design guidelines begin. Guidelines are "soft" rules for details not typically covered under zoning, and the degree of their compulsion and specificity can vary. The urbanist Denise Scott Brown believes that "guidelines should be evocative rather than prescriptive and should open opportunity and induce enthusiasm rather than constrict and smother." Others believe that guidelines need to be precise and strictly enforced if they are to be of any use at all.

The City of Vancouver, Canada, planning department often writes guidelines for development to accompany zoning text, such as the tower-top guidelines in its central district. These guidelines have real power because the overall approval for the development is discretionary by the people who wrote the guidelines. Failure to follow the guidelines adds substantial risk that a developer's plans won't be approved. The new neighborhoods of Vancouver are the products of specific requirements regarding materials and architectural details, applied at a large scale over a long period of time with a substantial degree of compliance. The results are extremely coherent new neighborhoods of very high urban design quality; however, the result is sometimes criticized for lack of visual variety.

"...guidelines should be evocative rather than prescriptive..."
—Denise Scott Brown

Guidelines, because they don't face the same high hurdle of enactment as zoning rules, can be a good place to experiment in urban design, piloting rules that may later become law in new fields. We can expect the focus of the guidelines to shift to topics of sustainability over specific building form as ecological imperatives come to the fore in city building. The ecological guidelines may take the form of solar zoning to determine building bulk, which permits optimum incidence of the sun, or the guidelines might be building-specific and cite performance standards over specifications and facilitate new forms of architectural expression. What began as "high-performance guidelines" for sustainability in New York are now becoming law through Zone Green.

There is a burgeoning convergence between health and sustainability in the built environment, and we are exploring the possibilities through active design guidelines. We had long advocated guidelines to make sidewalks walkable, but hadn't realized that what was good for design could be good for health. For me, the realization came from a meeting with Drs. Lynn Silver and Karen Lee of the city's Department of Health and Mental Hygiene, who had asked for our help to address what was the city's most important public health problem. The "obesity epidemic" had hit New York's children. Type II diabetes was growing rapidly and was beginning to catch up with the rate the rest of the nation was experiencing. This had enormous public health implications, both in diabetes's effect on these young peoples' lives and in their future productivity, and in its effect on ballooning health care budgets.

This was what Dr. Lee called "a disease of energy." More calories being consumed than expended leads over time to obesity and diabetes. It turns out that the simplest preventive is walking. And so our interest in the quality of the pedestrian experience became a health issue. Other agencies were enlisted and the

topic broadened to include all the aspects of healthy mobility and diet in the city. This was an outgrowth of the regular "Fit City" conferences we held, sponsored by the local American Institute of Architects, to define the policies and practices that came to be called "Active Design."

The capstone was the Active Design Guidelines, published in 2011, and five follow-on studies funded by the U.S. Centers for Disease Control and Prevention, including one specifically on the design of sidewalks. Led by my associate Skye Duncan, the premise of the sidewalk study is to place the pedestrian at

the intersection of sidewalk design and public policy. We begin with how people experience the sidewalk. We have gone beyond the rather dry analytic tools of plans and sections typical in urban design studies to think of the sidewalk as a *room,* experienced through motion within four planes defining its edges. We then catalogue the physical elements that make up each of the planes, much like an architect might draw the floor plans, ceiling plans, and walls of a room to specify the elements that make them up. Finally, we examine the policies that regulate each of these elements. These policies come from multiple agencies in complex overlaps of jurisdiction, and being able to parse these into mandates, guidelines, and incentives is essential to understanding our potential to improve the sidewalk experience in any neighborhood. This study provides a framework, not a recipe. You might say the study and its appendixes are a passionate catalogue of what we have found to be important in the design of sidewalks, supported by field observation both here in our native New York and via drawings of more than thirty successful sidewalks measured across six cities.

ROOF

ROADSIDE

BUILDING WALL

GROUND

The sidewalk as a room.

(Credit: New York City Department of City Planning)

URBAN DESIGN PRODUCTS: PLANS

The most common urban design product is a plan. Between the large scale of the regional plan and the small scale of the project plan lies a number of intermediately scaled plans in which urban design plays a major role. Whether defined geographically (metropolitan area, city, neighborhood, or district plan) or by approach (vision, community, resource, or process plan), all these plans might be categorized under the term "master plan." They become urban design plans when these larger planning goals are translated into products that can be understood experientially.

Urban planning sets out goals and quantities, but the look, feel, and function of the city—the way people live in it—is properly the province of urban design. At its heart a visual discipline, the power of urban design is that it communicates to everyone, lay or professional, a glimpse of what the city might become. If the vision is compelling, people will look and say, "I want to be there," which is the first step toward overcoming peoples' natural fear of change and achieving transformation. Urban design plans make the future visible.

Daniel Burnham made the phrase "make no little plans" famous when he uttered it to motivate support for building a temporary city of white plaster for the World's Columbian Exposition of 1893. "Make no little plans," he said. "They have no magic to stir men's blood and probably will themselves not be realized. Make big plans; aim high in hope and work, remembering that a noble, logical diagram once recorded will not die, but long after we are gone will be a living thing, asserting itself with ever-growing insistency. Remember that our sons and grandsons are going to do things that would stagger us. Let your watchword be order and your beacon beauty. Think big."[2]

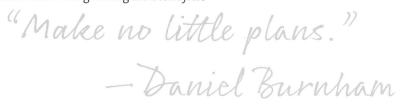

"Make no little plans."
— Daniel Burnham

But what exactly is a plan? Burnham's definition of "plans" in this instance combined an executive strategy to realize his designs, the designs themselves, and the result. Although the realization of Burnham's plan for the fair was temporary, it lasted long enough and was large enough for almost half the U.S. population of the time to wander through and wonder at the inspiration. The fairgoers returned home with an appetite to transform their hometowns in the image of Burnham's White City, with grand vistas and monumental public buildings.

The word "plan" comes from the Latin *planum,* meaning a level field, and also the tool that measures whether a surface is level. But plans can take many forms: two-dimensional maps to show the organization of space from above, flowcharts to show the steps necessary to accomplish work, three-dimensional scale models to give materiality to a conceived space, and the virtual reality of computer simulations. All of these are plans because they convey the intent of future reality, yet are not reality themselves. Perhaps we could say that all plans in urban design are proposals. With the construction of a life-size model of an entire quarter of a city that lasted almost a year before disintegrating, Burnham came as close to blurring the line between plan and reality as anyone has, although a popular urban design product today, the pop-up project, achieves the same result on a much smaller scale.

A pop-up project is a temporary taste of a possible future, such as San Francisco's Parking Day. On that day, members of the public take over a parking space and add planting, seating, and other amenities. For a day, the parking space becomes a tiny park. The cars return the following day, but anyone who enjoyed the benefits of the temporary park is more committed to greening the city than before.

Because plans are simply proposals, they are by far the most numerous of urban design products. Unlike rules, they do not require enactment; unlike projects, they needn't be built. Certainly, a few plans eventually become reality, but that success is rather independent of their production.

We make and review plans constantly at the Department of City Planning. Eventually, after long consultation among the stakeholders and the community, we may reach a consensus plan. That plan may eventually become part of the zoning code and zoning map. But it is rare that a plan is ever finished. At best what one can hope for is that the multiple iterations have distilled at least the essence of what it is we are trying to accomplish, and to quote Charles McKim, a colleague and rival of Burnham's, plans are a series of proposals that have the power to clarify urban design's intent; to be willing to compromise "everything but the essence."[3]

The Two-Dimensional Plan

The urban design plan as a two-dimensional representation is a kind of leveling tool, helping you compare options. Despite all of the computer tools available to see plans in multiple dimensions, designers often return to the traditional two-dimensional overhead view to make and record decisions. I believe this is because the two-dimensional plan has a certain objectivity to it, a lack of spin. But as an urban designer you need to have the ability to make a three-dimensional picture in your mind from a two-dimensional plan—to "read" city plans. This requires both a spatial aptitude and a feel for the conventions of urban design drawing, which imply much about

The New Plan of Rome by Giambattista Nolli, 1748.
[Credit: Accessed through Wikimedia Commons.]

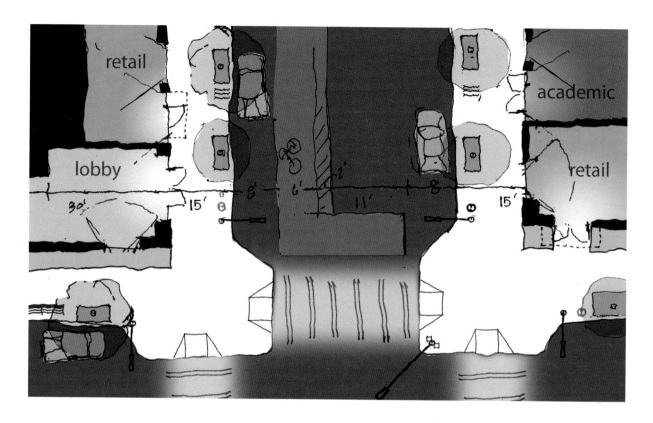

Strolli plan. *(Credit: Skye Duncan)*

the physical worlds without actually specifying it. Even so, it is always surprising how something as simple and spare as General James Oglethorpe's plan for Savannah, for example, can blossom into a place as complex and beautiful as that city today.

The sparseness of urban design drawings requires a focus on the information that is most important to convey. Giambattista Nolli's map of Rome from 1748 intended to show public space as the most important element; therefore, it left as white all spaces open to the public, whether outside in the streets or inside the churches and other public buildings. The result is a drawing that serves as a map of the public realm and a metaphor for the pedestrian's primacy. It is a plan that expresses a point of view—the pedestrian's—and records the values associated with it—public space. It served so well as an aid to public planning that Roman authorities used it as a base map well into the twentieth century.

The New York City urban design team wanted to update Nolli's mapping tool to take into account that the pedestrian realm no longer includes the full street, which is largely used by automobiles. To map the continuity and variety of the contemporary pedestrian experience, we developed what we call the "Strolli" plan, in which the degree of lightness of the color reflects the degree of public access. The Strolli plan puts the sidewalks, parks, crosswalks, retail spaces, and building lobbies—the places where pedestrians are free to stroll—in the lightest shade. Private spaces are dark, as are travel lanes in the streets. Everything that can be occupied by the pedestrian is dimensioned from the pedestrian's perspective, such as the clear path dimension on a sidewalk. In addition, all green items, such as tree pits and tree canopies, and all pedestrian amenities, such as benches, are drawn and dimensioned. The Strolli plan portrays the city as the pedestrian experiences it, and we use it as a planning tool to protect and enhance walkability in the city.

In the past, two-dimensional plans were limited to the information within their edges. With the development of geographic information systems, we now have the ability to easily reference more than one scale of plan at the same time, to go beyond the edges to link in network information. For instance, if we are proposing a form of drainage in a public park that can detain storm water in a series of landscaped weirs and bioswales, we can draw a plan that simultaneously references the park-scale elements with the watershed-scale hydrology. We no longer have to make design decisions that end at the edge of the page.

URBAN DESIGN PRODUCTS: THE PROJECT

The rarest urban design product is that of the built work—the project. If a built work can truly transform an area larger than its site and serve a community broader than its client, it can be said to be an urban design project. City-changing works of architecture, such as the Guggenheim Museum Bilbao, in Spain, are often cited as examples, but they succeed only if they are part of a larger transformative effort including infrastructure and economic and social development.

It is important that urban design projects be focused and targeted. To break the physical isolation of Santo Domingo Savio, a sprawling slum in Medellín, Colombia, that is home to 170,000 people, Mayor Sergio Fajardo realized he needed to provide public transportation. But the barrio was perched on a slope too steep for roads or buses (this is all too common that informal settlements take over land too wet or too steep to build on normally). Fajardo found a creative solution in a sky tram, like those that take tourists up Swiss mountains. Now the barrio is no longer physically isolated. Second, he put cultural and educational infrastructure for the entire city in the heart of the barrio, saying, "Our most beautiful buildings must be in our poorest areas."[4] Third, he co-located the sky tram stops and the cultural infrastructure in newly constructed green plazas of public open space. The urban design projects were targeted and coordinated for transformation.

A transformative project is very difficult to achieve because it requires sustained political, financial, and design agreement through all phases of work on a project from planning to execution. Usually, this is longer than a politician is in office or a market is in an upswing, and the project can die when the stars are no longer in alignment.

I would argue that built works of urban design are all, at a basic level, infrastructure—from the varieties of public space, including streets, squares, the hybrid "squeets" (see below), plazas, parks, and leftover space, to categories of the basic sanitary, communication, and transportation infrastructure that knits our cities together. Infrastructure is the trellis on which the vines of our civic lives grow. Without the support of infrastructure, any attempt to live at the density

Refreshed by a park in Edinburgh, Scotland. *(Credit: Skye Duncan)*

and richness of urban life would collapse in a heap of anarchy, filth, and disease. With innovation, urban designers can put infrastructure in the service of a larger sustainability agenda by demanding that infrastructure accomplish its engineering tasks in the context of adapting the city to the effects of climate change and mitigating the city's carbon emissions, as well as creating new public space resources that support the density required by growing cities.

But always remember how difficult it is to get a project built. Stuttgart's new high-speed rail station, approved in 2007, had as its goal to straighten out a major bottleneck in the main east-west high-speed rail network from Paris via Strasbourg and on to central Europe, correcting a legacy of nineteenth-century rail engineering in Baden-Württemburg. The plan puts the tracks underground, and through an ingenious roof system pierced with oculi to light the platforms, the station provides a roof strong enough to support the weight of a major new city park above it. The station is as much park as platform. It provides new open space for the city and a new, high-density, mixed-use neighborhood to grow over the old rail yard, repairing the center city's walkability damaged by the at-grade tracks of the previous century's station.

But will it be built? There are enormous cost overruns and serious political opposition, and the station's backers are experiencing the full fury of trying to go from urban design plan to urban design project.

The Street

> If you want to build a great city, build a great street.
>
> — *Rob Adams, director of city design, Melbourne, Australia*

A street is defined as the public right-of-way between private property lines. Every street on every block in Manhattan is mapped with a finite dimension between those property lines. That mapped space belongs to the public and can not be arrogated.

Within that mapped dimension, a multiplicity of functions must be accommodated. Some are underground, such as the movement of wastewater. Some are at grade, such as pedestrian mobility. A few functions are above the ground plane, such as lighting.

The range of functions we consider for streets includes pedestrian, bike, bus, automobile, truck, and rail transit mobility; it also includes pedestrian safety and sociability; light, air, and green space; storm water

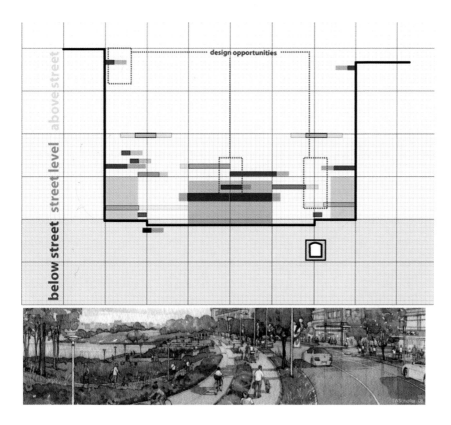

management; streetscape and architecture for place making; land use; and municipal services.

Each function is carried out by a specific built element; for instance, pedestrian mobility requires a sidewalk. Each function takes up space, and space is limited. Therefore, choices based on clearly articulated priorities must be made in laying out the street. The expression of those priorities determines which functions are accommodated, which functions are subordinated, and which functions are excluded. For instance, if a street has enough room for two car travel lanes *or* one car travel lane and a class 1 bike track, that decision must be made. Ultimately, the choice is an expression of policy. The transformation of Times Square into a pedestrian plaza is the most visible expression of New York City's policy to put pedestrians first.

The "Squeet"

There are certain public spaces that are both square and street. Times Square, for instance, functions as both. The Canadian designer Bruce Mau once described it as a "squeet." Traffic moves around the perimeter, and people lounge. The hybrid will become an increasingly important type of open space as pedestrians reclaim their place in the hierarchy of public space and stretches of right-of-way, formerly the exclusive domain of cars.

A model squeet: Times Square,
New York. (Credit: Janet Kao)

Plazas

Plazas are nodes of pedestrian open space connected to the street network.
Whether they are public spaces formed by the intersection of streets or privately owned but publicly accessible spaces fronting onto streets, plazas
are multipurpose outdoor rooms, destinations in their own right. Their
walls are formed by surrounding buildings or else infrastructure; their
furniture, such as benches or shade devices, provided as an amenity; their
social function determined by changing uses through the day and night.
Their only inalienable characteristic is that they are public space, open to
all, with no distinction made for income or any other arbitrary division
among people. Plazas are, therefore, places of pride for cities; no matter
how poor one's private rooms might be, as a citizen, everyone owns a share
of the greatest rooms in the city. The equity of public plazas is one of the
emblems of urbanity.

How can we technically define a plaza? Certainly a plaza has a high

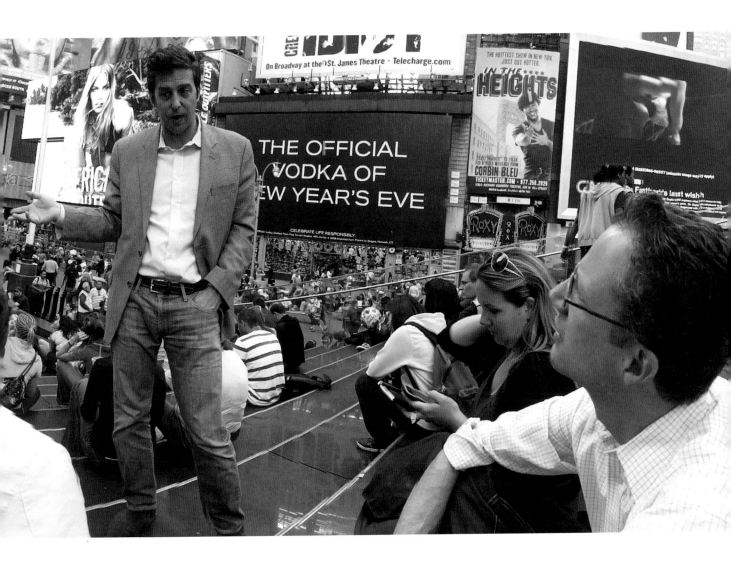

degree of hardscape—generally around 80 percent or more. Generally, there is social seating. William Hollingsworth "Holly" Whyte, the great observer of how people use public space, wrote many a careful observation in his book, *City: Rediscovering the Center,* in 1988. Many of those observations have been translated into regulations that New York uses to shape and maintain the privately owned public spaces (POPS)[5] that buildings have proffered over the years in exchange for bonuses in height or bulk. These privately owned public spaces are vital in New York. Sometimes called "vest-pocket parks," such as Paley Park in Midtown Manhattan (which was featured in Whyte's book *The Social Life of Small Urban Spaces*), or else conceived as architectural thresholds, such as the plaza in front of the Barclay's Center, these open spaces take on meaning through contrast with the crush around them. They have very carefully calibrated specifications for sight lines, planter and seat heights, even tread and riser dimensions—details all deemed necessary to maintain public quality in private space.

Parks

Parks are the open spaces where cities define their relationship to nature. I feel that parks are the most didactic urban design project, with the greatest range of vocabulary in their physical elements and the greatest opportunity for narrative in the sequence of their paths. Parks are ideal projects to mitigate the city's effect on climate, to adapt the city to climate change, and to educate citizens on the benefits of conceiving of the city and nature as one.

The twenty-first century brings a renewed concern for the environment and therefore a renewed sense of purpose for the urban park. The landscape architect and educator James Corner calls parks "ecological vessels" and sees three types of parks flourishing in the new urban context: big parks (e.g., Olympic Park in Beijing), productive parks (e.g., Landschaftspark in Duisburg-Nord, Germany, which remediated polluted soils through phytoremediation), and unique parks (e.g., Promenade Plantée in Paris, which was the inspiration for the High Line).

I see waterfront parks as particularly important to New York's future. In addition to their function of bringing people to the water, they can form a natural infrastructure of coastal protection and help lower the risk from flood to coastal neighborhoods.

For a park to be a work of urban design, it must transform the area around it, or at least the perceptions of the people who visit it. When connected, parks, plazas, and streets form a green network for circulation that creates a second city inside the first. Nature and city coexist. You can move effortlessly from one realm to another. In the twenty-first century, green can be ubiquitous in cities; you don't have to travel to Central Park, where nature is an "antidote" to the city. As cities consider ways of bringing nature in, designers might find that two small parks connected through the city by a street with newly planted street trees could be more effective than one large park.

Leftover Space

And what of those enormous spaces in every modern city, leftovers from the collision of transportation infrastructure with industry—the rail yards, the brownfields, the spaghettis of elevated train supports and highway overpasses? There is space here amid the transportation infrastructure; and space is at a premium in growing cities. How do we transform what is considered leftover and useless into a place that still works for transportation but has meaning to the citizen as a place of gathering? In New York we are experimenting with new forms that look very little like a traditional park. Queens Plaza, an unparalleled jumble of bridges, roads, and rails, has now become a place to stroll, without compromising the operation of the hard infrastructure around it. Nature is perfectly at home here; nature is infrastructure, too.

The concept of nature as infrastructure—connected, available, purposeful, even cost-effective—is proving itself at every scale. With limited sewer capacity, New York is piloting bioswale tree pits for storm water detention. And we are building greenways for biking, as in Brooklyn Bridge Park; fields for remediation of waste, as in Freshkills Park; and now after Hurricane Sandy, we

are thinking of nature as part of an infrastructure of coastal protection.

One proposal by Professor Guy Nordenson and the architecture firm ARO is a park constructed just offshore from Lower Manhattan. If you were to stand at the Battery and imagine Nordenson's proposal, you would see a series of islands in the harbor, lines of marsh grass, and shallow wetlands. The Statue of Liberty would stand in the distance over a bustle of activity nearby: people in waders, oystering, pleasure boats and ferries, school groups walking through trails in the marsh grass. In good weather, these new landforms in the harbor would make a wonderful new public park, but their resilience value comes from their performance during the one day a major hurricane might slam into New York Harbor, its winds concentrating billions of gallons of seawater through the Verrazano Narrows and pushing a storm surge toward Lower Manhattan. On that day, these islands and wetlands would act as a shock absorber, taking the lateral momentum out of the storm surge and protecting the neighborhood upland. At the moment it is just a plan, but we may find in the coming years that we need to muster the political, financial, and design resources to make it a built project, an example of the products of urban design that can make the city resilient while improving the quality of public life.

Rising currents. *(Credit: Courtesy of Guy Nordenson and Associates, Architecture Research Office, and Catherine Seavitt Studio)*

Rules shape the city in unseen
ways [Times Square].
(Credit: Skye Duncan)

Prioritizing transit modes.
(Credit: Douglas Moore)

Teardrop Park.

Battery Park City, New York.

(Credit: Alexandros Washburn)

Hong Kong building wall.

(Credit: Alexandros Washburn)

Athena on the High Line.
(Credit: Alexandros Washburn)

CHAPTER 4

THE PROCESS AND PRODUCTS OF THE HIGH LINE

When you correctly coordinate the process and products of urban design, you can transform cities. The High Line project and the Special West Chelsea District are successful examples of such coordination applied to the transformation of a neighborhood. In the timeline you can see the nested, iterative process of urban design where politics, finance, and design intersect. You can see how the same process of designing the question, designing the solution, and then implementing the solution plays out almost simultaneously at every scale and across every product of urban design. Whether it is a rule (e.g., the policy change to support reuse of the High Line or the zoning text establishing the rules of the Special West Chelsea District), a plan (e.g., the economic study or the final design), or a product (e.g., the opening of the first section of the park or the construction of the HL23 building and the transfer of its remaining air rights to build 100 Eleventh Avenue), the process of urban design was used to make the transformation happen.

You can see which products of urban design played what role when. See how Joel Sternfeld's pictures in the *New Yorker* overnight redefined the "client" from being a few Friends of the High Line to a million people across the world who saw what the High Line could become. See how the Department of City Planning's special district redefined the "site" from just the land under the structure itself to an entire New York City neighborhood. See how the air rights transfer mechanism changed the "program" from building a $100 million public park to triggering $2 billion worth of new private buildings. Each product of urban design was a discrete, actionable instrument to shift the ground, to change the rules of the game, to make transformation happen.

THE STORY

The High Line is a massive, four-track elevated freight railroad that runs down the west side of Manhattan. It was built in 1934 as part of Robert Moses's West Side Improvement project to increase the efficiency of deliveries to the industrial buildings of West Chelsea and to once and for all solve the safety problems on Tenth Avenue, where Cornelius Vanderbilt's original railroad tracks still ran at grade. Tenth Avenue had been nicknamed Death Avenue for all the pedestrians hit by trains, and the High Line solved the problem by lifting the train tracks twenty feet above the street. The High Line also brought trains directly into the second floor of many of the processing plants and refrigerated warehouses of the neighborhood, which

in the 1930s served as the city's meatpacking district.

In today's dollars, the High Line cost more than $1 billion to build. Barely thirty years after its construction, it was obsolete for transportation. The rise of refrigerated trucking and the transportation afforded by the new Interstate Highway System meant that meatpacking was more efficiently done outside the city. The industry began to leave West Chelsea, and the multistory warehouses emptied. The last train to use the High Line moved three boxcars of frozen turkeys in 1981. After that, the rail line was abandoned.

A few meatpackers hung on in the old neighborhood, working their predawn trade in the desolate landscape, while the area around Gansevoort Street began to attract sex clubs and an underground club scene. The hours of the neighborhood were the reverse of most everyone else's: the meatpackers and clubs and prostitutes all worked the night shift. The daytime visitor saw only an eerie wasteland of very slow decay.

The area's decay began to attract artists and those who cater to them. Florent Morellet rented a diner near the abandoned rail line in 1986 and opened Restaurant Florent, which became a social focus for the neighborhood. Artists converted a loft building into a cooperative. In 1994 Matthew Marks opened the first high-end art gallery nearby; scores of others followed.

Along with the artists came land speculators. Some of the cheapest land was directly under the elevated rail structure. They bought the land under the rail line, and rented it for parking. As the galleries started to improve the tone of the neighborhood, the landowners started lobbying the city to remove the High Line so that they could build on their parcels of land. The zoning allowed them five stories. With the structure removed, they could make a pretty good profit. They had the ear of Mayor Giuliani, and the city began to process the demolition order.

Unused, the High Line structure had long ago faded into the background, a silent mass of steel hovering above the street, its abandoned roadbed snaking through the neighborhood. At a community meeting to consider the demolition, two young local men happened to sit next to each other. Both had been intrigued by their neighborhood landmark, the giant steel structure sprouting trees. But neither had thought much about it until they realized it was threatened. They didn't know what the structure could be used for, but they had a hunch that demolition was the wrong thing to do. Robert Hammond and Joshua David decided to do something about it. They formed an organization called the Friends of the High Line (FHL).

They got permission to walk the roadbed from the corporation that owned the tracks. The site was strange but beautiful; the structure had gone to seed over the last two decades, and trees and wildflowers grew in silence where the trains had once run. Hammond and David began to bring their friends up to see. I was lucky to get one of their early tours and to help organize a mediating session to convince the landowners to rethink their position. But the FHL really gained momentum when pictures by the famous photographer Joel Sternfeld were published in the *New Yorker* magazine, introducing millions to the hidden strip of nature that had taken root above the rail line. Suddenly people could see the potential.

Hammond and David simultaneously developed their political connections, their financial structure, and their design ideas. They organized an international ideas competition to help visualize what the structure could become. They found that more and more people wanted to help; they held fundraisers and increased their donor list.

Mayor Giuliani's term was almost over, and the FHL were racing the clock to beat the demolition order. The turning point came when the new mayor, Mike Bloomberg, appointed a Friend of the High Line, Amanda Burden, to chair the city's Planning Commission. The demolition order was rescinded, and the city and the FHL now faced the question of turning the

Transfer of development rights. The new zoning designated a High Line transfer corridor and receiving sites for air rights from land under the High Line. *(Credit: New York City Department of City Planning)*

vision into a reality: what to do with the structure, the owners of the land beneath it, and the neighborhood around it. And of course, how to pay for it.

The process started with an economic development study to look at the costs and benefits of turning the structure into a park. The study determined that the investment in renovation would be more than returned in taxes. But what could be done about the landowners who still wanted to tear it down?

The answer was zoning. Burden made the project a first priority for the Department of City Planning and charged the staff with developing a strategy to link the renewal of the High Line with a renewal of the neighborhood. In so doing, she intended to devise a process that would let the landowners realize the value of their land while dropping their demands for demolition.

The result was Article IX, Chapter 8, Section 98 of the New York City Zoning Code: the Special West Chelsea District. The general purposes section laid out the goals of the project: to transform the High Line into a unique linear park; to provide new housing for the neighborhood; to preserve the character of the existing art gallery district; to add a mix of uses to the neighborhood; and to ensure that new buildings were shaped to enhance light and air to the new park and to fit in with the surrounding neighborhoods.

The existing zoning was ripe for rethinking. The district had remained zoned for manufacturing decades after manufacturing had left. Art galleries were permitted in these zones, hence their recent invasion into the cheap and airy spaces.

The new zoning map would keep these uses in the center, maintaining the manufacturing designation to protect the character and scale of the arts

district. But the area around the perimeter of the neighborhood would be changed to allow residential land uses as of right. Together with ground-floor retail typical in New York apartment buildings, this would provide the mix of uses necessary to keep the neighborhood vibrant 24/7.

Zoning regulates building bulk as well as land use. Now that land use would change to allow residential apartment buildings, the question became how big would these buildings be? New York has a chronic undersupply of housing, so new residential buildings are highly lucrative to developers. They wanted the right to develop as much as possible.

Here is where the rezoning solved the problem of how to satisfy the economic interests of the owners of the land under the High Line and remove their opposition to the park. The definitions section created a High Line Transfer Corridor, defining it as "the area within which the High Line is located, where development rights may be transferred to receiving sites." The receiving sites were in the new residential perimeter. The owners of the land under the High Line could sell their development rights to these developers, let the High Line stand, and make a smart profit.

There was so much demand for the development rights that the zoning could include a tool to increase the neighborhood's supply of affordable housing in the same deal. In addition to the transfer of rights off the corridor,

Transfer mechanism used by the Department of City Planning. *(Credit: New York City Department of City Planning)*

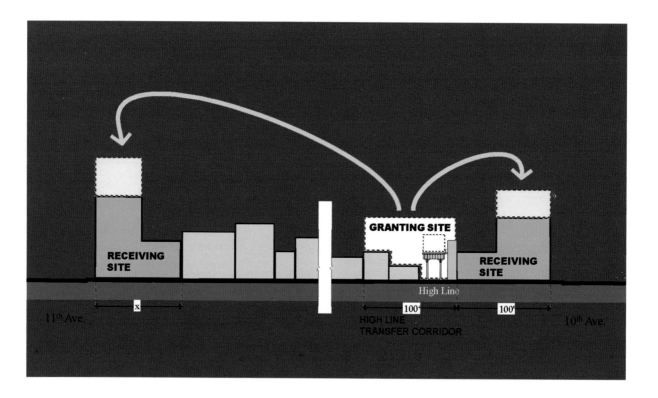

the zoning permitted a bonus of 30 percent more development rights if the owner developed 20 percent of the building as affordable housing. This worked to make the neighborhood more diverse, to become mixed-income as well as mixed-use, and to help whittle down New York's affordable housing shortage.

The demand for development rights was strong, but the ultimate size of the buildings in the receiving site was limited by the need to ensure light and air for the park as well as to fit in with the surrounding neighborhood. The zoning designated several subdistricts of varying densities to tailor the bulk to the surrounding neighborhoods—for instance, the large-scale development to the north and the small-scale development to the east. The special district map came to look like a mosaic.

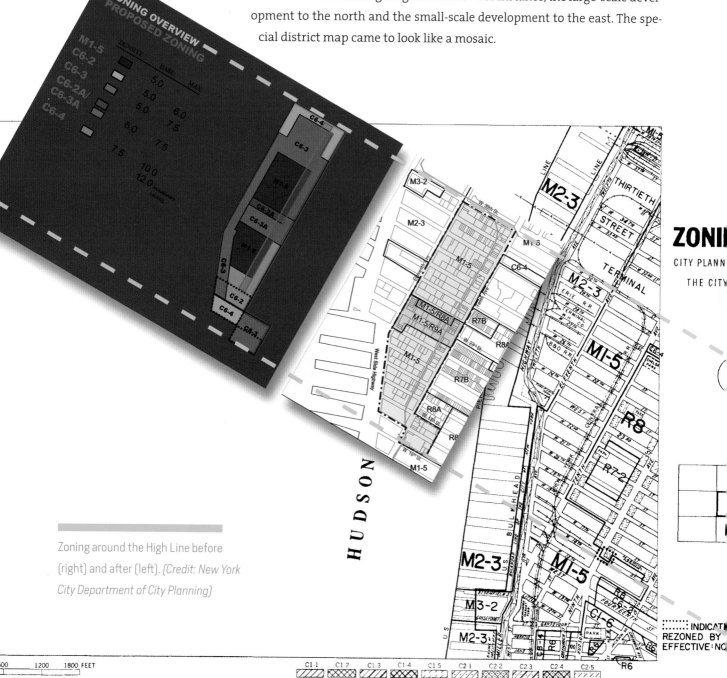

Zoning around the High Line before (right) and after (left). *(Credit: New York City Department of City Planning)*

However, density limits alone were not enough to ensure light and air to the new park. Here the geometry and sun angles were so complex that the zoning needed to come up with special rules for buildings adjacent to the High Line. These adjacencies would largely determine the character of the experience in the new park. To explore what those rules should be, the City Planning Department drew options, over and over, by hand and by computer. Should buildings touch the structure? What uses should be at eye level? When should buildings set back?

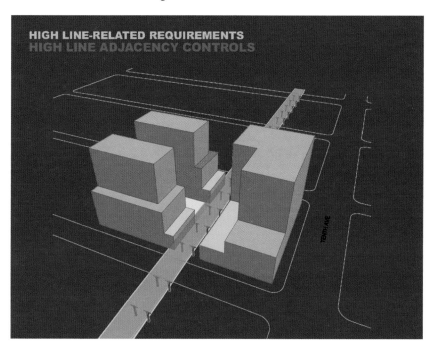

HIGH LINE-RELATED REQUIREMENTS
HIGH LINE ADJACENCY CONTROLS

Eventually these decisions were codified as special height and setback regulations. For instance, one lot would have a requirement of 20 percent open space landscaped at the level of the High Line. Another would require a fifteen-foot setback for 100 percent of the frontage along the High Line. When you put all these requirements together, you got a building form that cradled the High Line.

The **special district** didn't happen overnight. The zoning change took three years between the economic development study and final passage of the special district. But the process of negotiating the terms of the zoning itself aligned the interests of the stakeholders with the overall vision. The process of endless drawing and modeling of potential scenarios kept the language specific and purposeful. When the zoning finally passed, it was like a starting gun went off.

Because the FHL had prepared a world-class design for the landscape of the park, their insistence on quality set a very high standard for the design of the buildings around the neighborhood. When it came time to build, developers enlisted some of the world's top architects for their commissions. You can see how the zoning worked if you look at two of the

zoned for manufacturing but was now allowed to be residential.

He hired Neil Denari, a cutting-edge Los Angeles architect, to design a top-of-the-line, for-sale condominium building for him adjacent to the High Line. Because of bulk limitations meant to keep buildings adjacent to the High Line in proper scale, the Denari building could not use up all the development rights

neighborhood's signature buildings, HL23 by Neil Denari, and 100 Eleventh Avenue by Jean Nouvel.

If the High Line had been demolished as the landowners originally wanted, a piece of land at 511 West Twenty-Third Street would have become a five-story warehouse midblock between Tenth and Eleventh Avenues. It consisted of lots 27, 28, and 43. Immediately after passage of the rezoning, the developer Alf Naman formed a limited liability corporation to buy these lots that were in the High Line Transfer District. He also formed a corporation to buy a piece of land on Eighteenth Street at Eleventh Avenue at the perimeter of the special district, which had before been

on-site. So the developer transferred the remaining rights to other sites, including 15,000 square feet to his development site on Eleventh Avenue. That site was being designed by Jean Nouvel, the Pritzker Prize–winning architect from Paris, as an apartment building. By transferring the rights, the Nouvel building could be larger, and the development rights could be used higher up, in the tower of the building, which made them even more valuable.

Value was being created at every step of the process. The original owners of the land under the High Line got a satisfying value for their land, more than they would have gotten had they succeeded in tearing down the High Line. The Denari building got extra value by being next to the High Line. (Several times when I've walked past it on the High Line, I've seen people point up to it and say they wished they lived there, on the top floor. It's become a landmark.) The Nouvel building got the extra value of the tower floors, and put some of that value into its spectacular, extravagant facade. Even the dark space under the High Line got value; the developer is allowed to buy one floor of development rights back from the city to build a shop or gallery under the structure and thereby make sure there aren't any gaps in the streetscape below. But the greatest value created by the Special West Chelsea District was for the public now able to experience a new perspective on New York that married urbanity and nature, for whom this transfer mechanism resulted in the preservation of the High Line and the creation of the unique, linear park.

Jane, Bob, and Fred

I wonder how my three favorite New York urban designers would view the High Line. I know that Robert Moses would be impressed by the numbers. In the first five years alone since the rezoning, nearly $2 billion of private investment has poured into the neighborhood. Twelve thousand jobs have been created, more than half of the 2,500 apartments and half-million square feet of commercial space has been built, and every year brings more construction. Moses would have been impressed—yes—but he also would never have believed that something so big could have been started bottom-up by two local guys who met at a community meeting.

Even the dark space under the High Line got value.

Jane Jacobs would approve of the neighborhood's fine grain of cafes and galleries, the success of its street life and the mix of old and new buildings that preserves the neighborhood's character and attracts new residents. But Jacobs would have been suspicious of government's role in the transformation. I doubt she would have believed that a planning agency could have made rules sensitive enough that the character of the neighborhood would improve rather than degrade during the transformation.

Finally, I think Frederick Law Olmsted would find a walk down the High Line as refreshing as a ramble through Central Park. But he would think we were crazy to build the park twenty feet in the air.

The project time line shows the process and products of urban design that helped to make Hammond's and David's idea a reality.

Start the Process: State the Problem and Establish a Point of View

In 1999, to counter the efforts of a group of landowners to demolish the High Line, Hammond and David form an advocacy group called Friends of the High Line. They do not know exactly what the elevated structure should become, but they follow their instincts that demolition would be detrimental to the neighborhood.

In 2000, the efforts of the FHL are publicly opposed by Mayor Giuliani, his chair of City Planning, and a coalition of land speculators, including the largest parking lot operator in New York City. Energized by their underdog status, Hammond and David spend the next year organizing membership to their group and are successful with both a grassroots and celebrity appeal, attracting to their cause actors such as Edward Norton, Jr., and fashion designers such as Diane von Furstenberg. Opposition politicians also flock to the cause. Amanda Burden, a City Planning commissioner, becomes a Friend of the High Line. Gifford Miller, a city councilman, becomes a Friend of the High Line.

In 2001, the *New Yorker* publishes Joel Sternfeld's photographs of the nature of the High Line in an illustrated article, "A Walk on the High Line," giving the reuse of the structure international publicity (May). The Design Trust for Public Spaces, a not-for-profit advocacy group, recognizes the potential of the FHL vision. It first organizes a forum with city, state, and federal government officials to explore the political, financial, and design feasibility of an adaptive reuse of the structure (June). The second move is to appoint a design trust fellow to produce a research and outreach report called "Reclaiming the High Line."

In 2001 Michael Bloomberg is elected mayor (November). Recognizing the growing momentum of the FHL, outgoing Mayor Giuliani signs a demolition order in his last days in office (December). A lawsuit (Article 78) is brought by the FHL, the Manhattan borough president, and others decrying the city officials' move to demolish the High Line without a Uniform Land Use Review Procedure.

1999

2000

2001

Products: A Policy Framework and Economic Development Study

In 2002 Mayor Bloomberg assumes office. He appoints Amanda Burden chair of City Planning. Gifford Miller is elected chair of the City Council. The City Council passes a resolution advocating the reuse of the High Line (March). The City's Economic Development Corporation issues a study showing that reuse of the High Line is economically feasible and will generate more tax revenue than the cost of construction (October). The Department of City Planning begins to study how the tools of zoning can support a reuse. The city makes reuse of the High Line official policy by filing a motion with the federal Surface Transportation Board (December). The New York State Supreme Court rules that the Uniform Land Use Review Procedure should have been undertaken before reaching demolition agreement for the High Line, thus officially staying demolition (December).

More Products: Rules and Plans

In 2003, City Planning Department staff begin to develop a framework to integrate a reuse of the High Line structure with a redevelopment of the surrounding neighborhood. The neighborhood is currently zoned for manufacturing, in the center of which a thriving art gallery scene has begun to grow. The department staff study how the potential development sparked by a new High Line park could be shaped to create a mixed-use neighborhood to accomplish a variety of the city's goals. A study area is delineated and, based on the findings of the earlier economic study, the goals of a rezoning are stated to provide market-rate and affordable housing opportunities in West Chelsea, to facilitate proposed open space along the High Line, to enhance the existing gallery district at the center, to encourage a dynamic mix of land uses around the edges, and to ensure the form of new buildings relates to neighborhood character and proposed High Line open space.

The landowners who had lobbied for demolition continue to oppose the rezoning, until a solution is found to increase the value of their interests. With a technique of air rights transfer similar to that which saved Grand Central Terminal from demolition, the rezoning studies allowing landowners under the High Line to sell their air rights within the study area. To provide a place to "land" these air rights, the rezoning would create taller "bulk envelopes" around the perimeter. The allowed use of these air rights would include residential and commercial space, which have higher values than the landowners' existing permitted manufacturing use.

In 2003, the FHL holds an open ideas competition for design concepts for the High Line. More than seven hundred designers from around the world respond. Ideas include using the structure as a nature trail, light rail transport, and (one of the winners!) a two-mile-long swimming pool (July). The ideas are exhibited and serve as a warm-up to a smaller competition to follow to pick the designers of the actual project.

The rezoning process looks at how to shape the bulk envelopes to achieve the goal of protecting neighborhood character and preserving views, light, and air to the new park. In countless meetings with stakeholders, community groups, and officials, staff try iterations of possible rules, drawing by hand and computer, to come up with suitable adjacency controls for the shape of the new buildings. These rules have to adapt to a further increase in bulk when the rezoning comes to include mechanisms to provide more affordable housing. "Inclusionary zoning" is mapped onto certain sites, allowing a developer 30 percent more development rights for providing 20 percent affordable housing on the sites. Finally, realizing that if the proposed rezoning is successful and a landowner under the High Line transfers away all the air rights, the land under the High Line would be bare, the planning department adds a provision to allow a buyback of a small amount of space. In this way, galleries or shops could be built under the High Line and keep the street life continuous, rather than interrupting it with vacant lots.

In 2004, the FHL and the City's Economic Development Corporation conclude a design process, selecting James Corner Field Operations and Diller Scofidio + Renfro, along with Piet Oudolf as the designers of the proposed park (September). The city commits $50 million to construction and launches the design phase of the work.

In 2004, the rezoning is certified to enter into the Uniform Land Use Review Procedure, and the sequence of public hearings and votes begins.

In 2005, the Uniform Land Use Review Procedure on the rezoning is complete. The City Council votes for and the mayor signs documents adding Article IX, Special West Chelsea District, to Chapter 8, Special Purpose Districts, of the Zoning Resolution of the City of New York (June). The rules are now in place.

In 2005, preliminary design work is complete and is exhibited at the Museum of Modern Art (April). Structural design and bidding of the drawings continue over the following year.

2004

2005

2005

2006

2008

2009

2010

2011

2012

Build the Public Project

In 2005, the city is issued an interim certificate for trail use by the Surface Transportation Board (June). Ownership of the High Line structure is transferred to the city by CSX railroad (November).

In 2006, ground is broken for the first section of the High Line (April). Two years of heavy construction follow.

In 2008, landscape construction and planting begins.

In 2009, section 1 of the High Line park opens to the public from Gansevoort Street to West Twentieth Street (June 9).

In 2010, in less than a year since opening, the two millionth visitor arrives at the park (April).[1]

In 2011, section 2 opens to the public, from West Twentieth to West Thirtieth (June 8).

In 2012, the High Line had more than 4.4 million visitors, becoming the city's most-visited park per acre.[2]

Cofounders of Friends of the High Line Joshua David and Robert Hammond on the third section of the High Line before its completion. *(Credit: Photo by Joan Garvin courtesy of Friends of the High Line)*

Develop Private Projects

The development of private projects around the High Line did not have to wait for the park to open to the public. The city's ownership and commitment of funds to build the park, coupled with passage of the special West Chelsea rezoning, was sufficient to spark redevelopment. By the time the second section of the park opened to the public, more than twenty-eight projects totaling two million square feet were already complete using the mechanisms put in place by the rezoning. An example of the timeline for private building can be found by following the public records for two pieces of land where air rights transferred from one to the other and whose developer built two outstanding buildings, one called HL23, by the architect Neil Denari, and one called 100 Eleventh Avenue, by the architect Jean Nouvel.

In 2005, a limited liability corporation purchases the lot underneath the High Line on the north side of West Twenty-Third Street, less than one month after enactment of the West Chelsea rezoning (July). Preliminary review drawings for a development called HL23 are submitted to the City Planning Department (November).

In 2006, 34,520 square feet of air rights are transferred off the site (January).

In 2007, developer Alf Naman releases drawings of 100 Eleventh Avenue and begins construction (April).[3]

In 2008, air rights transfers are completed (November). Naman announces the start of construction on HL23 (April).[4]

In 2010, Naman completes 100 Eleventh Avenue (June).[5]

In 2011, Naman completes HL23, which opens in June to coincide with the opening of the second section of the High Line below it (June).[6]

2005

2006

2007

2008

2010

2011

The High Line as experienced from an
apartment above. *(Credit: Jeff Shumaker)*

Skye drawing on the High Line.

(Credit: Alexandros Washburn)

Watching the world go by on the High Line. *(Credit: Douglas Moore)*

Summer on the High Line.
(Credit: Alexandros Washburn)

Old and new on the High Line.

(Credit: Douglas Moore)

Kayaking from Brooklyn Bridge Park.
(Credit: Alexandros Washburn)

CHAPTER 5

URBAN DESIGN FOR GREATER RESILIENCE

Transformation is the everyday business of urban design. In this closing chapter I examine the specific urban design strategies that can guide our cities' growth to be sustainable and resilient. I propose a framework for evaluation of these strategies—a set of "ecometrics" that can help make real-time urban design decisions in support of long-term environmental goals. Project examples are examined from around the world that incorporate those strategies in their designs, leaving each city better adapted to its environment, more resilient in its operation, and more creative in its generation of resources, and in the process, richer in its civic life. And finally, I come home to Red Hook, Brooklyn, and ask if those same strategies can change my neighborhood, too.

The techniques of resiliency depend on two related but distinct sustainability strategies. Mitigation is a strategy to reduce the probability of adverse changes in the climate system by reducing the concentration of greenhouse gases (carbon dioxide equivalent [CDE]) in the atmosphere. Adaptation is defined as "initiatives and measures to reduce the vulnerability of natural and human systems against actual or expected climate change effects."[1] The two are related by a risk equation, as we will see below in the section on ecometrics. But the broad point is that they work together and both are important: mitigation works to lower the probability of future climate change risk; adaptation lowers the consequences to us from climate change that is already happening. Adaptation can be thought of as the virtue of prudence, taking protective steps such as building a seawall or making wise investments in physical or social infrastructure that make a city more resilient. Mitigation can be thought of as the virtue of thrift, saving money and resources by changing our behavior and equipment to consume less, because today virtually all consumption results in the release of greenhouse gases.

MITIGATION

Urban design is involved if the mitigation strategies used to reduce greenhouse gases can also transform the city to improve the quality of civic life. For instance, if the technical goal is to raise the mode share of walking relative to driving and thereby reduce overall carbon emissions from transportation, an urban designer might suggest improving the quality, amenity, and connectivity of sidewalks. A successful mitigation strategy is relatively easy to measure technically because we are calculating the reduction of a physical quantity, such as metric tons of carbon. The strategies to achieve it vary by city, but the primary targets are to increase efficiency in the energy used by either buildings or transportation. Of course, buildings are connected by transportation, so how far away you put them, and how you connect them, are important. Their distance from each other, and how many floors stack up in each one, are measures of density.

Mitigation through Increased Density

Those who don't like density quip that the best way to mitigate is to move to California. This refers to the fact that in a pleasant climate such as California's, not much energy is needed to heat or cool buildings, so being

wasteful in other ways, such as living in a sprawling autocentric community, doesn't matter so much. In places where the outside temperature is close to the desired inside temperature, buildings consume less energy and emit fewer greenhouse gases. San Diego, a classically sprawling California city of suburbs, has an annual per capita CDE rate of 12 metric tons, quite thrifty compared to the U.S. national average of 26 tons.

Yet Barcelona, a city with a mild Mediterranean climate not dissimilar to San Diego's, has a per capita CDE rate of only 4.2 tons. Why the difference? Barcelona has a dense compact urban form with great walkability and high use of public transit. Buildings in Barcelona and San Diego don't use much energy because of their climate; Barcelona's transport system doesn't use much energy because of the city's shape. It's dense.

A 2009 study found that doubling the density in a city from about ten to twenty people per acre corresponds with a 40 percent reduction in greenhouse gas emissions. The numbers aren't hard—climate and topography and the availability of public transit must be taken into account—but overall the point is clear: walkable density reduces emissions from vehicle travel.

Being nominally antidensity can lead to the worst of both worlds: dense sprawl. For example, São Paulo, Brazil, has a maximum density of four times the lot area across the city. (By New York standards, this is pretty low; we have parcels reaching a density of thirty times the lot area.) Therefore, in order to build the popular high-rise towers, a developer must

assemble huge lots, most of which remain unoccupied so that overall density measures remain low. But these lots are gated and unavailable to the public; often they are used for parking. The public mistrust of high density in São Paulo and its density cap, intended to benefit citizens, instead crowds out parkland at the ground plane and forces the city to spread out in a dense, gated sprawl to the point where a commute can reach several hours and there is little feel of either openness or continuity to the pedestrian.

If density is done right, it can be appealing even in a society that is used to sprawl. Christopher Leinberger, research professor at the George Washington University School of Business, has surveyed attitudes about density among urbanized Americans and found that roughly speaking, a third want to live in the suburbs and can't imagine life without a car, a third want to live in dense areas and want to be able to walk everywhere for their necessities, and a third don't care either way—they will go for whatever is cheapest.

Leinberger interprets these results less as a victory for one typology or the other than as a declaration that more than anything else, people want choice. I would agree, but I think that the possibility of their living choices being curtailed scares people into hardening their affinities for one or the other—low or high density—walkable or auto-oriented. Given the high CDE of low-density, auto-dependent development, global suburbanization could have disastrous results for climate change mitigation efforts. Supporting this assessment, the Lincoln Institute of Land Policy reports that the world's fastest-growing cities expanded spatially much faster than they did in population, meaning that the global trend is against density, not toward it.[3] If some sizable percentage of the world's urban population wants to live in the suburbs, we have to ask how we can satisfy the demand and still mitigate the earth's carbon dioxide. Is there a way to make suburbs sustainable? Using the techniques of urban design, I would also ask if we can make suburbs more livable, with better public space and a higher quality of life, not just lower emissions.

Suburbia is trying its hand at city-ness by retrofitting auto-oriented infrastructure to denser patterns. Successful shopping malls are becoming "lifestyle centers" with Main Streets and ancillary housing built on decks over shops and parking. Greenways for bikes and bus rapid transit lines for commuters, originally innovations from Latin America, are finding their way increasingly into suburban areas that want some of the transportation conveniences of density but don't have the capital for or population to support subway transit.

Density is a tool of mitigation; it is not an end in itself. The larger point is that density has to be likable, and people like variety. Suburbs need not be uniformly low density and cities need not be uniformly high density to be successful. Variety itself is a valid goal.

New York City values variety; a surprising number of our neighborhoods are "suburban" in density and visual character. Yes, Midtown Manhattan has building parcels with thirty times the floor area of the underlying lot, but other boroughs have building parcels with only 0.3 times the area. With respect to density, this is a variety ratio of more than one hundred to one.

Offering options for living in different types of neighborhoods is the underlying strategy that helps to make New York one of the most sustainable cities in America. All these different densities share in the city's infrastructure, making even the low-density areas more efficient than their counterparts in the suburbs. The range of densities gives people the choice of living in a skyscraper apartment building in Manhattan or a single-family home with a two-car garage on Staten Island, while every gradient of density in between can be found in Brooklyn, Queens, and the Bronx. Of course, some of those options are more expensive than others, and to help with the issue of equity we apply an affordable housing bonus to new development. In certain well-transited areas, the city will grant developers 30 percent additional density to their buildings in exchange for the inclusion of 20 percent affordable housing.

If density is done right, it can be appealing even in a society that is used to sprawl.

Mitigation through Transit-Oriented Development

Walking is the healthiest, lowest-carbon form of transportation. But walking works primarily at the neighborhood scale. As a strategy for mitigation at the scale of today's mega-cities, walking can not do it alone. Pedestrian mobility needs other, faster forms of transportation to link multiple walkable neighborhoods together in a way that can handle the millions of trips in a modern city while mitigating CDE.

Today all major cities contain a mix of three transportation modes. The automobile is a reality, mass transit is a necessity, and the efficiency or pleasures of a truly walkable city are hard to dispute. The historical, path-dependent layering of these three types of city is contributing to the growth of what are called polycentric cities, in which dense neighborhoods (call them "nodes" if you want to sound technical) are connected as much to each other as to the vestige of an original downtown. A strategy of densifying today's polycentric cities is called transit-oriented development (TOD). The amazing energy efficiency of transit—the New York City subway emits little more CDE than the city's street lights—makes TOD the prime tool in the strategy of mitigation through density.

You could say that TOD is the DNA of New York. By committing to building subways as the preferred mode of transit in the early twentieth century, New York committed to orienting its development around them. Even though Robert Moses grafted a network of highways into the transit mega-city that was New York in the 1950s, and the zoning code was amended in 1961 to accommodate the automobile, the subways have held their own. Today more than seven million people a day use the subway; meanwhile, automobile use has peaked at a fraction of that. Slightly more than 700,000 vehicles enter Manhattan on a busy day.

If you look at a map to see where we plan to accommodate the next million New Yorkers, and then look at a map of our subway infrastructure, they match up. We want to increase density where there is already the transportation capacity to support it, so we "up-zone" (meaning we increase the density by adjusting the floor-area ratio) where there is transit, and we "down-zone" where there is not. This shows that the strategy of TOD can work to maintain open

Growth in New York City (top) is planned around existing and planned transit routes (bottom).
(Credit: New York City Department of City Planning)

space in a city by concentrating growth in dense, walkable neighborhoods. We thereby protect the character of the lower-scale neighborhoods where cars are a necessity by not allowing development that would overwhelm their existing road system. The goal is to make the overall city more resilient by channeling growth to the transit nodes, but the up-zone/down-zone policy makes the overall city more attractive by providing choice in housing types.

Of course not every city has the benefit of a mass transit system, and subways are expensive to build. The answer may be bus rapid transit, in which articulated, high-capacity buses run on dedicated rights-of-way. It is a mode of transit that combines the low capital cost of buses with the predictability of subways. Bus rapid transit was successfully implemented in Curitiba, Brazil, by mayor Jaime Lerner, and cities as diverse as Istanbul and New York use it today.

...the New York City subway emits little more CDE than the city's street lights...

Like the subway system, New York is facing real challenges to its resilience. In 2008, a short, sudden rainfall overwhelmed the city sewer system and water poured into subway tunnels. We responded with a "raise the grates" program that lifted subway grates five inches high. This was one of our first successful forms of urban design adaptation. Lifting the grates solved the technical challenge of flash flooding, and we designed them to act as a pedestal for benches and bike racks, so they also improved the quality of the public space around them. A small victory for sustainable urban design. But during Hurricane Sandy, a thirteen-foot–high seaborne storm surge overwhelmed the subway tunnels under the East River. We weren't prepared. The subway shut down, so the city shut down. Somehow, we have to increase the resilience of our old subway system, because we can't reduce our dependence. The subway system is the backbone of New York's urban development, and we are committed to it in the way we pattern density and a mix of land use throughout the city based on transit's capacities.

In planning for TOD, we should remember the last mile. Subways and buses don't drop you at your doorstep. Transportation planners call this the last-mile problem. Whatever the exact distance to a final destination, it must be walked. New York has always seen this trek from subway to

Grates and bicycle parking before (left) and after (right).
(Credit: New York City Department of City Planning)

doorway as an opportunity. The improvement of the city's pedestrian network is a top priority, and we spend a lot of energy improving the quality of public space where people walk. In some ways, increasing walkability is New York's most important mitigation effort. Without a pleasant—and safe—walk at either end of the journey, fewer people would use transit. The police department makes the streets safer. In my work, I try to make them pleasant and functional to walk down. Previous chapters detailed the elements that go into designing a pedestrian network that functions with great amenity (sidewalks worth singing about). The bottom line is that walkability leads to sustainability, and TOD allows a mega-city to function as a polycentric city, a web of walkable neighborhoods. A striking example of successful TOD in New York is the Bank of America (BofA) Tower at Forty-Second Street in Manhattan. Like the Chrysler Building, another great skyscraper down the street, the BofA Tower is rooted into transit, with an entrance into the subways built into the entrance of the tower. The symbiosis with the subways is a New York tradition, and the city often encourages buildings to improve the subway stops that serve them by offering a transit

bonus, a zoning incentive to allow a building more density in exchange for improvements to the transit system.

The mitigation effect that the BofA Tower achieves as an example of TOD is clearest when you compare a suburban option for the same two million square feet of office space that are in the tower. The Metropolitan Transit Authority, which runs the subway, wanted to calculate[4] the avoided CDE of such a development when you take into account the energy used by workers commuting to it. In the tower, you have one very tall building with no parking; in the suburban condition, you have ten shorter buildings with more than 1.8 million feet of paved area for cars—almost as much of an area for parking as for the office space itself. The tower is more efficient with respect to CDE in the materials required for its construction as well as the energy required for its operation, but only marginally so if the suburban buildings are built with the same insulation, light shelves, and other green building design tactics as the tower. The significant difference in energy use and therefore CDE comes when you factor in the commute of the workers inside. According to the Metropolitan Transit Authority study, the

tower and its transit commuters use 41,000 BTUs per square foot per year, and the suburban office park and its gasoline-powered auto commuters use 201,000 BTUs per square foot per year.

Mitigation through Better Building Design

Buildings can mitigate CDE by working together as well as by working with mass transit. By coordinating buildings with their neighbors to make a backdrop for a great walkable street, building design can aid mitigation by making density more attractive.

Buildings can create great, walkable outdoor space by forming its edges, coming together to make an outdoor room, a public space. In architecture school, this public space is called "negative" space to connote the area not occupied by buildings. But it should be called "positive" space because it is an addition to an extremely valuable resource: well-designed public open space. The technique of designing individual buildings to cooperate with other individual buildings to form a continuous backdrop for the public to enjoy civic life outdoors is the art of making what is called a street wall. This can be as elaborate as the Place des Vosges in Paris or as simple as a street lined with market stalls in Hong Kong. If an architect treats his or her building less as an individual object and more as a member of a chorus of other buildings, an outdoor room for public use can be created with the facades collectively.

Building design can aid mitigation by making density more attractive.

Individually, buildings are far more energy-efficient today than they were a century ago. The global green-building movement has been successful, in part, because energy-efficient buildings are not only sustainable, but cost-efficient over time given lower nonrenewable energy needs. Energy-saving techniques of controlling light, insulating walls, and planting green roofs are becoming second nature to the architects of new buildings. Guidelines for these techniques and scoring systems for their achievement can be found all over the world. The LEED (Leadership in Environmental Energy and Design) system started in the United States; Abu Dhabi has Estidama; the United Kingdom has BREEAM; the Indian Green Building Council has a variety of standards for homes and public buildings; and China has a green building labeling system. New, even more integrated approaches are developing from these initial standards, such as the Living Buildings Challenge,

Bank of America Tower, Manhattan.
(Credit: Alexandros Washburn)

which looks closely into not only a building is built but monitors how it performs over time.

We could not have gotten from the energy-wasting single-pane skyscrapers of the *Mad Men*–era to net-zero buildings today without such standards and guidelines. But there is more than a whiff of bureaucracy in these endeavors. Standards soon become dogma, especially when administered by large, national boards, and there is always the danger that in checking off the boxes to get the maximum score, you miss the bigger picture of how buildings can make the world more sustainable. Yes, buildings must be more efficient in how they use energy. But they must also be built in the right place, in the right relation to their neighbors, with the right program, and their designers must be open to emerging concepts of sustainability, such as biophilia and biomimicry, which blur the distinction between natural and man-made and support the notion that nature and the city are one. These are evolving areas of practice.

Today, however, the best climate-change miti-gation strategy is to put your biggest buildings at your densest transit nodes and make the buildings as energy-efficient as possible. The BofA Tower, mentioned above, is a real-world success at very large scale of an energy-efficient building in a very dense area on a transit node.

The BofA Tower is fifty-five stories tall and contains more than two million square feet of usable space on a lot that takes up about half of a city block. It has a variety of spaces, including a public plaza, a restored historic Broadway theater incorporated into the structure, giant unobstructed trading floors, a sky lobby, numerous basements, high-speed elevators, and acres of rentable commercial space, all topped with a spire visible for miles in any direction. The architect Bob Fox was under instructions from Douglas Durst, the building's developer, to make it green. It's the first megatower to achieve a LEED platinum rating and, when designed, it exceeded the requirements of the energy code by more than one-third.

The building uses numerous mitigation tactics to

Hong Kong market street.

(Credit: Alexandros Washburn)

reduce its carbon footprint. It has a basement ice farm that uses electricity at night to chill water that is then used to cool the building during the day. It has an insulated curtain wall facade with frit patterns etched directly into the glass to provide shade, and automatic louvers behind them. The glass is coordinated with light shelves to throw sunlight deep into the floor plates, reducing the need for electric lighting, one of the biggest users of power in a building. Electric light draws power in its own right, but it also generates heat, which then requires more power to run an air conditioner to cool the space it's in. The building distributes hot and cold air through a raised floor, making microcontrol of individual work space temperatures feasible. The developer took space in the building and experimented with a true double-glass facade around his corner office. The technique forms a narrow greenhouse around the space to insulate it from the heat and cold outside; it is an eerie feeling to stand in the narrow slot between two panes of glass hovering a thousand feet over Manhattan's streets.

The building could have been even more efficient if not for our own city and state regulations. For instance, Durst included a cogeneration facility, a high-speed turbine that could turn natural gas into electricity at a fraction of the CDE per unit of energy that the power company requires. It could generate enough power to run the building and even pump excess capacity back into the grid, taking the load off our aging infrastructure with distributed power generation. However, a tangle of fire code regulations and sly pricing by the power company have kept the building from generating all the resources it could. At a meeting with city officials where we complimented him on the extraordinary sustainability of his building, Durst pleaded, "Change the rules so this kind of building will be ordinary." The conversation made me think that a long-term goal of building design for sustainability is to change the terms of reference so that it becomes commonplace that every building gives something back to the city, that every building be designed to produce renewably a portion of the resources it consumes.

Even though new buildings can be wonderfully efficient, the rate of building replacement in the city is such that new buildings cannot account for enough improvement in a short enough time. The only way to reach our carbon mitigation goals this generation is to come up with retrofit solutions for the existing stock of buildings.

The obvious part of retrofitting buildings to increase mitigation is new, more efficient mechanical equipment and better sealed and insulated building envelopes. The vertical faces of a building envelope, the facades, have always performed multiple duties: insulating, lighting, shading, ventilating, allowing views, creating character, and also forming the street wall, the backdrop for the textured and dynamic experience for the pedestrian walking down the street. In New York, a combination of zoning rules and building code interpretations had come to favor increasingly thin-skinned buildings that reduce the role of the facade to a container for conditioned space. We are working to change that through a series of zoning and building code modifications to permit increased depth and articulation. A building facade is not just a container for the space inside the building; it is the backdrop for the space outside the building as well.

"Change the rules so this kind of building will be ordinary."

—Douglas Durst

Changing mechanical systems in existing buildings is the other primary mitigation tactic. Sometimes this is as simple as switching the combustion chamber on a boiler to run on natural gas rather than a particularly dirty grade of fuel oil popular with New York landlords because it is cheap. Other solutions rely on sensors to turn on and off lighting and conditioning equipment as spaces are being used; still other solutions rely on clever techniques of chilling a building's structure to cool it or recapturing energy from lighting to heat it.

The real problem in retrofitting buildings is coming up with the right incentive. There is no limit to the imagination and expertise that a mechanical engineer can provide. There is a limit, however, to what building owners will spend to retrofit their buildings. Without a carbon tax or fuel pricing that includes all the externalities, energy costs remain too low to justify building owners' return on most capital-intensive retrofits. We need to come up with other ways to incentivize retrofits. Perhaps a zoning bonus, perhaps a tax abatement. The successful mitigation strategy for changing existing buildings will come at the intersection of policy, finance, and design and therefore is very much in the province of the urban designer.

Mitigation through Resource Creation

The conversation with Douglas Durst made me think that another way for buildings to reduce their net emissions is to produce a portion of the energy they consume. It is representative of a mitigation tactic called resource creation. It works not by reducing but by replacing. A building can create energy renewably with a solar panel, and this replaces energy produced by a fossil-fueled power plant. We then might consume this energy to run our air conditioners without the guilt of emitting carbon. The Danish architect Bjarke Ingels calls this "environmental hedonism." He delights in making large-scale projects that seek to balance consumption with resource creation. Ingels is young, optimistic, talented, and rather free of guilt. He is the opposite of the dour "zero-impact man" of contemporary Brooklyn, whose beard, flannel shirts, and home-cured meats signal an impulse to live off the grid while living in a fourth-story walk-up flat. Ingels puts a charismatic face on what I feel may be one of the greatest strategies for mitigation while still improving the quality of life. He uses the creativity that is in abundance in cities to innovate ways of making food, water, power, and even land, so we can live more richly in cities while substituting those resources that otherwise emitted greenhouse gases. Tactics such as these can range from the megascale "ride the wind" idea that the Metropolitan Transportation Authority looked at to build a series of offshore wind turbines whose electricity would power the subway to simple retrofit solutions such as the Brooklyn Grange's rooftop farms. Somewhere in between is my house in Red Hook, on which I would

like to put solar panels to handle the summer peak load of my air conditioning while I enjoy a blueberry or two from my roof garden.

Through estimates of capacity, resource generation tactics can also be applied to urban design rules, such as a zoning change to allow vertical farming as a land use in a district, or bulk limitations, which ensure a certain amount of sunlight can reach a park. To analyze a building for opportunities of conservation and generation is a relatively straightforward exercise. Not surprisingly, much depends on the spatial characteristics of the typology. For instance, don't expect a green roof to do much to the eco-metrics of a skyscraper; it's just too small an area relative to the total area of the building. But a green roof on a row house can do wonders; it can be a third of the area of the house. A very useful exercise is to take a common building type in the city, quantify how much energy can be saved through conservation via insulation, shading, and equipment efficiencies, and then evaluate how much energy can be generated through surfaces available for solar and wind power and the capacity for geothermal heat exchange in the lot area on which it is built. It will show that every building is capable of generating a portion of the resources it consumes, depending on the characteristics. As a bonus, it should be noted that resource creation in cities also has a mitigation correlate: every resource created locally does not need to be transported from afar. Therefore, it should get a mitigation credit for avoided carbon emissions from obviating the need for transport. Even transmitting electricity, because of resistance in the transmission wires, has a mitigation penalty. The longer the distance traveled, the lower the percentage of generated electricity is available to power its target. So if the electricity is generated locally and only travels from the rooftop solar panel to the room air conditioner, that's efficient.

The mitigation tactic of resource generation relies on creativity; you have to be clever to make something out of nothing. You could even say that the High Line project is an example of resource creation. In effect, the project created new parkland without using actual land. It combined the creativity of two community activists with a disused elevated rail line. The result is a new resource for the city: parkland. Creativity is an abundant resource in any city because cities draw creative, energetic people to them. Translating that individual creativity into resource generation at the scale of buildings results in a powerful principle: every building should generate a portion of the resources it consumes. Could this become a zoning rule? This would provide an incentive simultaneously to reduce overall energy consumption and increase renewable resource production in a city.

Mitigation through Carbon Capture

To conclude our discussion of mitigation requires consideration of the technique of sequestration. Also called carbon capture, sequestration is seen as a magic bullet form of mitigation that, if successful, would reduce emissions, but not change the pattern of cities. Carbon capture is a technical fix, but it is not urban design because it seeks to maintain the status quo rather than change it.

For instance, some people believe that carbon-capture devices can be engineered to remove greenhouse gases at the smokestack so that even coal-fueled power plants could have negligible greenhouse gas emissions into the atmosphere. In turn, the electricity they produce could heat and cool our existing high-energy suburban homes and could charge the nation's cars if they were made battery-powered. With these technical fixes in place, the greenhouse gases that come from the current fossil fuel-powered land use and transportation patterns of sprawl would be obviated.

There are other unsustainable aspects of sprawl, such as inefficient land use and a lack of accountability in the costs of infrastructure and other externalities. A suburban lifestyle currently results in substantially more carbon emissions than a dense urban lifestyle, and that needs to change.

But if it changes because of a technical fix, so be it. The emissions argument against suburbia would go away (perhaps to the chagrin of those who cast the issue as a moral argument). One major caveat: beware of those who claim such technology will be here tomorrow, and we therefore need not change today. Their promises are likely protecting an entrenched interest, not the environment.

ADAPTATION

Although we can speculate about mitigation strategies that work toward reducing carbon emissions and the probability of future climate change, cities urgently need adaptation strategies to reduce the consequences from climate change that has already occurred. For some cities the issue is drought; for New York it is floods. There is urgency to adaptation that I have felt in the flooding of my own house and neighborhood, urgency that the city feels from the track record of two years in a row with forced evacuations and subway shutdowns, urgency that the state and federal governments feel with massive bills to pay for the damage of the last two storms. These were supposed to be one-in-a-hundred-year storms, or by some calculations, one-in-five-hundred-year storms. Yet they occurred back to back. What will next year bring?

It is only prudent that we adapt. But how prudent is prudent enough? No city can take every precaution and be absolutely secure—it's a statistical impossibility. So putting in place the right amount of adaptation requires us to measure risk. In adapting for flood, we have to balance the risk of chronic changes, such as sea-level rise, with acute events such as hurricanes. Sea-level rise has high probability, but its consequences year by year may be measured in inches. A hurricane has low probability, but if it hits, its consequences are immediate and devastating. It is prudent to adapt for both, but measures that might work individually, such as raising a berm along the shore to a level above the new sea level, may not work in conjunction. A storm surge coming off the new, higher sea level could easily overtop the berm.

Where you adapt matters as much as how you adapt. Because adaptation is always carried out locally, prudence requires understanding the city itself better. Staff of departments of planning or emergency management need to understand their city from the point of view of a climate change event. Which part is most vulnerable? Which infrastructure is most critical? Which community is least resilient? Each adaptation action of fortification, resilience, or retreat is a specific, local countermeasure. The problem of climate change may be global, but the adaptation response is always local, and the better a city knows itself, the better it will be able to make specific adaptations that lower the most risk for the least effort.

Adaptation in cities has three basic tactics: fortification to harden edges; resilience to bend but not break; and retreat, to move out of harm's way. Having seen my own house flooded, I would argue that the best strategy combines elements of all three. Moreover, I would layer those defenses at multiple scales. Precisely where a hurricane might strike, the angle at which it might be moving, and the state of the tides at the time it strikes will largely determine the extent and location of damage. Quantifying these probabilities and identifying adaptation measures to counter them requires advanced techniques of risk management, not just weather reports. In New York, an archipelago situated at the confluence of several political boundaries and diverse watersheds as well as ocean, estuary, and river systems, the calculations are complex and the response is shared across many governmental units. The city's Department of Emergency Management works out our contingency plans, but it has to coordinate with the Federal Emergency Management Agency and the National Oceanic and Atmospheric Administration to try to understand the hydrodynamics of potential storms. These efforts are aided by local institutions, such as the Davidson Lab of the Stevens Institute of Technology, which places sensors in New York Harbor and has real-time web-based maps of the rate, direction, and salinity of water flows in New York Harbor. All of this provides an enormous amount of information to manage with enormously important decisions to be made about what and how to prepare. My hope in combining the scales and tactics of adaptation is to diversify our response, share risk management across a spectrum of responses, and avoid the surprise stochastic event—the "perfect storm" that would otherwise overwhelm our best-laid plans.

The problem of climate change may be global, but the adaptation response is always local.

Adaptation through Fortification

When roving bands of vandals in the chaos of the crumbling Roman Empire threatened the capital of Constantinople, the emperor Theodosius
built walls to fortify the city against the risk of sacking. In much the same
way, the City of London, when faced with the threat of floodwaters coming
up the Thames from the sea, lowers the flood gates of the Thames Barrier.
It is an act of fortification, a tactic to harden the edges. In London, to date, it
has worked. If the fortifications hold at the barrage, there is no need to el-
evate buildings or build them to withstand flood. But rising sea levels and
increased intensities of storms have the authorities in London contemplat-
ing a larger barrage, farther downriver. The city depends on its fortifications at the perimeter in order not to flood in the interior. Perhaps London
will be as fortunate as Constantinople. It took almost one thousand years
for the fortifications there to be breached.

Ten thousand years is the standard the Dutch use in judging their fortifications. These fortifications are against water. The Netherlands, the "Low
Countries," has 21 percent of its population living below sea level. To prevent a disaster such as the 1953 flood, which killed almost two thousand
people, the Dutch have built more than 1,800 miles of seawalls and 6,200
miles of dikes in a formidable system of federally planned fortifications.
These fortifications are at the largest scale, and because they are in place,
smaller scales of cities and buildings need not be fortified to the same extent. The Dutch have calculated the cost and the odds, and determined that
fortifying the perimeter with national resources at the regional scale is the

most effective and best-value tactic to prevent disaster from a storm event.

Fortification can also occur at the smallest scale. You can dry flood-proof a building by creating a waterproof perimeter to protect space below the flood level. In New York, we allow dry flood-proofing only for commercial space; we don't allow residential space to be built below the flood line. But this is often ignored in practice, and in many existing buildings the basements have been illegally converted into apartments, putting their perhaps unsuspecting tenants at great risk. So if individual buildings can't be fortified, the next possible scale to fortify would be the block scale. A clever solution is to preinstall foundations for a temporary seal wall around the perimeter of a block. When a storm event is forecast, residents would evacuate and trucks would bring around steel wall panels and drop them into the foundations, protecting the houses during the flood. After the storm, the wall panels are removed and the residents return, hopefully to dry homes.

Adaptation through Resistance

The second major tactic of adaptation is to build in a resistant manner that can temporarily accommodate the damage a storm brings. The approach can be as simple as using flood-resistant materials, or we can engineer buildings for passive survivability, meaning that we incorporate areas of refuge into the designs. We can move temporarily into these areas, which are either hardened or elevated, and provided with some sort of food, water, and energy reserves that let us get through the storm and bounce back.

Social Adaptation

Bending but not breaking is not just about physical adaptations; it can be social too. São Paulo, Brazil, is vulnerable to riverine flooding. It is built in an upland plateau at the foot of the Brazilian Highlands and has sprawled to straddle the Pinheiros and Tiete Rivers. Storm water drainage is complicated by the rampant informal construction of favelas on the steep slopes and even in the beds of tributary streams. To cope, São Paulo has built massive underground cisterns to capture runoff from the heavy seasonal rainstorms. The entire system is monitored by video and operated via a twenty-four–hour command center.

But the technical adaptation is not addressing the root problem, which is social. São Paulo is a great city; its population is similar to that of New York, and like New York, it is a magnet for strivers, for the best and the brightest of the entire continent. It is fascinating, dynamic, rich—for those who succeed. But the divide between those who succeed and those who don't (or haven't yet) is vast. From the helicopter, the city is a fascinating quilt of luxurious towers and hyperdense favelas, cheek by jowl. From the street, all you see is a wall. Walk through the garbage and flooding of what passes for a street in the Paraisopolis favela and you reach a wall. On the other side is a private tennis court. Above you looms a strangely blank white tower. It is only from the helicopter that you can see that behind the turned-up edges of each balcony on the tower is a private swimming pool for every apartment.

There is social unrest, and the residents of São Paulo fear rising crime and violence, with an average and mostly illegal gun ownership rate of one per seventy-five residents. The leading cause of death among youth is homicide, and youths make up the largest segment of the city's population. One-third of the city lives in favelas where the police have less control; in the neighborhood of Cracolandia, high-rise buildings have in the past been taken over by

Paraisopolis, São Paulo, Brazil.
(Credit: Alexandros Washburn)

gangs, tagged with graffiti, and filled with squatters.

To reduce the city's vulnerability to climate change shock, it may be more important for São Paulo to increase its social resilience than its physical resilience. In a time of climate stress, having a society in which different groups of people are fearful and distrustful of one another is a weakness that intolerably raises the risk of climate shock. Adaptation in such a context requires breaking down the boundaries between rich and poor and increasing the confidence in government. The chief challenge is a retreat from the violence and prejudice of the present, and the first step is to acknowledge the humanity of the parties and put a "face" on the problem, as the artist JR did when he plastered huge photographs of residents' faces on the walls of a favela in Rio de Janeiro.[5]

The people and government of São Paulo know that the lack of social resilience is a problem, and they are working to overcome it. But how? São Paulo has set up an organization under the secretary of urban development, SP Urbanismo, to carry out urban design adaptations that also serve as social adaptations. It is currently focused on two strategies for bringing infrastructure into existing favelas or building new housing blocks in brownfields and demolished favela areas. SP Urbanismo and COHAB, the city's housing agency, are going into the favelas to connect them to the metropolitan infrastructure and raise the quality of housing stock. In Heliopolis, they channelized a portion of the street, landscaped it, and paved the remainder. What was an open sewer is now a functioning street, and the shacks lining it are now more solid houses. Unfortunately, there are now high security walls along the street, but connecting to the city is real progress. It is producing a quality result, improving the flood control system, and helping to knit the favela population into the larger city. But it is slow work, and the question is whether it can keep up with the astounding demand, estimated at one million units over the next fifteen years.

All cities have vulnerable populations, and social adaptation is a strategy that can limit the consequences of climate events in each of them. Eric Klinenberg, a professor of sociology and director of the Institute for Public Knowledge at New York University, has studied the effects of severe heat waves on statistically similar populations in Chicago, finding that networks of social cohesion are vital to surviving extreme events, especially for the elderly.[6]

Adaptation through Planned Retreat

Given the growing understanding of the danger of flooding, some wonder why cities don't simply retreat to high ground. The people who think this way, including some environmental regulators working at the state or federal level, do not understand the immense financial and emotional investment a city makes in its location.

Generally speaking, major cities are sedentary and proud of it. Their populations do not retreat. Their capital gets reinvested in their buildings and infrastructure over generations. Looking at the example of Istanbul, despite wars, invasions, plagues, and droughts that have beset it, its permanent population never considered wholesale retreat or abandonment of the city. Indeed, the city has remained in place under different empires and different names: Byzantium, Constantinople, Istanbul. Today it is once again one of the leading cities of the world, the largest city by population in Europe. However, Istanbul faces the question of retreat at the neighborhood scale. Today's city contains many "gecekondu" or "overnight" neighborhoods, some of which have been built illegally in floodplains. They are in harm's way; indeed, in 2009 more than thirty people died from flash floods engendered by the constriction of drainage channels caused by these settlements. The remedy, though very difficult politically, would be to remove the neighborhoods. But if you walk through the neighborhoods, they seem like any other, with stores selling fruit spilling onto the street, women hanging laundry from lines and calling their neighbors. The sense of danger is not palpable. Yes, the neighborhoods were built somewhere prudence dictates they should not have been. But retreat is a bitter pill. When people come to settle, they come to love their neighborhoods, and relocation is very difficult to carry out voluntarily. In the borough of Staten Island, New York City is experimenting with government buyouts of vulnerable property. Certain

A favela in São Paulo, Brazil.
(Credit: Alexandros Washburn)

cities, such as Dhaka, Bangladesh, give their redevelopment authority broad powers of possession and demolition for government intervention. In other cities, involuntary demolition may not be politically viable and engineered solutions may cost more than poorer cities can afford. What will happen to the Istanbul residents who live in the floodplain of the Astanya River if they stay? To move may be anguish, but to stay may be fatal.

Around the world, neighborhood retreat is a problem disproportionate to the poor. Many of the slum neighborhoods of the world are located on cheap, marginal land that did not have any value for development, often because it was so exposed to the dangers of flood or rockslide. Whether the land was then settled legally or illegally is often a question of the distant past. For example, the Providencia favela in Rio has been occupied informally for more than a century. There is no clear solution. The difficulty in moving neighborhoods from harm's way is a conundrum that will only grow more pressing with increasing climate change.

At only one scale are retreat tactics of adaptation relatively easy to achieve: the building scale. Here, getting out of the way means bringing residential occupancies and critical utilities upstairs out of the flood zone. If a storm surge of ten feet is calculated as likely for an area, then making the ground floor a use such as retail and not housing makes sense because you can always rebuild and restock the store's shelves when the floods subside. Electrical panels and furnaces can be moved upstairs, where they may be able to function when the power is restored. Ground-floor construction can include knock-out panels to get out of the way of rushing water without transmitting lateral forces to the structural frame.

Freeboarding, or raising the first occupiable floor above the floodplain, is a proven way to avoid flood. In many beach communities, for instance, it results in a neighborhood of houses on stilts and people tend to park their cars underneath. But raising a building in such a way in more built-up, urban neighborhoods is very problematic. First is the question of cost when buildings are made of masonry, and practicality, when buildings are attached and share a party wall. You can't just raise one attached house without raising its neighbors. But another problem with freeboarding is what it does to the streetscape for walkability. If the activity in buildings is raised more than a few feet above the sidewalks and replaced with parking, walking down the street becomes a bore. The social life of streets is threatened. The enormous strides we have made in livability in New York over the last generation could be threatened in safety if we no longer have "eyes on the street"; in economic development, if we have parking where once we had stores and apartments; in affordability, if the ground floor of row houses can no longer be rented out to defray the cost of a mortgage and insurance; in public health, if we retreat from our devotion to walking down varied and lively streets. This is one case where making a neighborhood only resilient to flooding

may degrade the quality of civic life, and it is a design question we are struggling with citywide.

A desire for change gives a city the opportunity to make things better or worse. Ecometrics let a city keep score. Urban design has to manage a process of change; therefore, urban design requires a series of metrics. We can not manage what we can not measure, so if we accept the challenge of changing cities to improve the quality of civic life while simultaneously mitigating future climate change and adapting to climate change that has already occurred, we need a system of measurement that can act as a reality check on our process. Call the system ecometrics, and define it broadly enough to make urban design accountable both to the realities of science as well as to the intentions of our value system to make cities both livable and sustainable. Use it as a guide to make choices among actions that make our city more resilient and reduce our carbon emissions, all while making room to grow and simultaneously improve the quality of civic life. Ecometrics should help us decide what changes are worth what effort at what cost and for what benefit. Ecometrics should yield transparency and strip away the fuzziness of mere good intentions. The sorts of urban design decisions we have to make to change our cities are expensive, pervasive, and of long duration; they will affect generations to come. If we make them wishfully, with no system of metrics, relying only on our good intentions, we risk paving a road to hell straight through our neighborhoods.

Ecometrics can simultaneously and quantitatively evaluate both mitigation strategies as well as adaptation strategies. I hope that its measures could potentially be integrated into the better-established notion of triple bottom line accounting, which seeks to evaluate a decision's effect on "people, planet, and profit." But the ecometrics I am imagining are not immediately suited to the accountant's ledger. They require integrating abstract strategies of risk avoidance. Mitigation, which deals in quantities of greenhouse gases not emitted, and adaptation, which deals with climate disasters avoided, are both successes if nothing happens. Both have different units of measure as well as processes of measure, the former hypothetical, the latter stochastic. Where they are related is through the notion of risk.

$$Risk = probability \times consequence$$

New York City has a higher hurricane risk than New Orleans. Though the probability of a hurricane strike is lower, the consequences, because we are a larger city, are higher. Ecometrics would use the risk equation to set up a decision-making relationship between mitigation and adaptation. Mitigation can be understood to affect probability: it can lower the index of greenhouse gases in the atmosphere and thereby eventually help reduce the energy in the weather system and decrease the likelihood of future extreme weather events. Adaptation can be understood to affect consequences: a seawall might protect a city from a given storm surge. If my neighborhood had had a fourteen-foot–high seawall, there would have been very few consequences from Sandy's storm surge. Of course with increasing greenhouse gases, the likelihood of the next storm surge being higher than fourteen feet is greater. Therefore, adaptation and mitigation are linked. The shorthand equation might read:

$$Risk = (probability - mitigation) \times (consequence - adaptation)$$

So if we want to manage climate risk, everything we do should be designed to either lower probability or lower consequences. In other words, if there is no mitigation today, any adaptation will be overwhelmed tomorrow. But by writing equations, I don't want to imply that a mathematical system of ecometrics currently exists; it does not.

We have components of such a system, such as the carbon counts New York and other cities take annually to monitor their mitigation efforts. We have predictive wave models and flood insurance rate maps made by governments and private insurers. We have algorithms such as HAZUS, which the Federal Emergency Management Agency uses to estimate the consequences of likely storms. But we have nothing to integrate all that we know quantitatively at the biggest picture level.

A system of ecometrics is most useful if it first is normalized across categories of sustainability strategies of both mitigation and adaptation to facilitate meaningful cost-benefit comparison for any combination of rules, plans, and projects. Single-purpose projects are expensive; convergent projects such as the Marina Barrage, discussed later in this chapter, which create resources, mitigate, and adapt all at once, are a much better value to cities but are difficult to calibrate for maximum effect. With ecometrics, we can balance among the sustainability strategies in a project logically and avoid wasting resources on red herrings.

With ecometrics, we can balance among the sustainability strategies in a project logically.

Second, ecometrics ideally will be able to measure both the scale of the problem and a city's capacity to respond. We were interested in New York City's solar capacity, so we calculated the amount of roof area in the city and its orientation and amount of sunlight it received. Adding solar panels to roofs would increase our mitigation, but would that preclude us from making blue roofs that detain storm water and therefore could be an important adaptation to protect our sewer system in case of short, severe rain storms? How would giving over the city's roof area to solar panels affect our ability to make green roofs and produce food, as Brooklyn Grange does on top of several industrial buildings? What percent of an urban asset—roofs—should go to what sustainability strategy—mitigation, adaptation, or renewable resource creation—and who should decide? Ecometrics should give us a basis to make such choices, and not necessarily in a top-down manner. Ecometrics is a natural for cloud sourcing.

Finally, because sustainability is a multigenerational project with targets that can change (for instance, sea-level rise may be more or less than we currently expect), ecometrics needs to assess our relative progress over time, answering how much closer we are to reaching our goals with each generation striving to transmit the city better and more sustainable to the next generation.

Although a functional system of ecometrics does not exist, I believe that such a system is entirely possible. My optimism stems from work we are doing with Eric Sanderson, the scientist who used geographic information systems to marry techniques of forensic cartography and habitat ecology to make a detailed computer model of Manhattan four hundred years ago, before the arrival of the first Europeans. Sanderson has been applying similar techniques to a new project: a cloud-sourced model of possible ecological futures for Manhattan. We wondered what our island would be like four hundred years from now. Could it be sustainable? That simple question led Sanderson to create a model to track stock and flows of water, carbon, biodiversity, and population.

The information architecture behind the model is specifically what gives me hope that a system of ecometrics is within our reach. For this first version, Sanderson divides Manhattan into a grid of cells with thirty-three-foot resolution. Each of those cells can be "painted" with a ground cover by users on the web as they make models of what they might like the city to become. This cloud-source input goes into a system of calculation that links the type of use in each cell (which can range from skyscraper to forest) with the kind of lifestyle of those populating the city (from original Lenape Indians to contemporary average Americans) with a variety of climate scenarios. Each variable is linked to a set of parameters, and the values for each parameter are searchable and transparent as to how they were determined. From the output of a solar cell to the average biomass of a pet, there is a reference that can be checked and, if necessary, improved, à la Wikipedia. There are more than eight thousand parameters, and their recombination with the two hundred variables on a half million cells might boggle the mind, but not the computer. It's all trackable. Beyond the rigorous specificity of his database, the genius of Sanderson's model is that he uses interrelationships among species and habitat to make predictive changes to the model ecosystem. It is called a Muir web diagram. The same technique of mapping relationships that Sanderson used for Mannahatta in 1609 to predict that where you find a beaver you will likely find a stream with certain fish and trees with certain bark and certain insects and so on he uses in Manhattan 2409 to predict that if you choose to place an apartment building on a certain cell and populate it with a certain type of people you will get a certain ecology. With cloud-sourced inputs, the results are instantly visible as the server calculates each user's model in real time and displays both the image of the hypothetical city as well as a dashboard of its basic ecometrics of water, population, carbon, and biodiversity.

One very brilliant person (Sanderson) with a Rockefeller Foundation grant and a small team of researchers has made a model of a prototypical system of ecometrics. I sense that a practical system that can be used in making day-to-day political, financial, and design decisions is entirely possible. The city and its information can be one.

GLOBAL EXAMPLES OF MITIGATION AND ADAPTATION

The effectiveness of urban design to increase resilience is gaining momentum. The purpose of urban design is not just to meet the technical problems of flood and carbon emissions but to improve the quality of civic life in the process. A growing number of projects around the world are achieving that purpose. Some projects address social adaptation, some increase resilience to rainfall, some lower carbon emissions by making bicycling a viable alternative. The projects range in cost from almost nothing to billions of dollars, some operate at the scale of small communities, others are part of a national infrastructure. But whether it's children playing soccer where once there was sewage or businessmen dipping their toes in a river between meetings, all change a city in a way that improves the quality of public space and therefore public life.

I describe a few possibilities below, less to catalog best practices than to encourage you to look for examples in your city. I look at the Marina Barrage project in Singapore, a major built work of urban design that has managed to transform risk into reward

for that city, and it makes me think of a new approach to resiliency in which the reduction of climate risk might actually prove financially lucrative. I close with thoughts on how we can do something similar to make my own neighborhood resilient.

Kibera: A Community Adapts

In the slums of Kibera, in Nairobi, Kenya, danger comes from something as commonplace as a strong rain. One section of Kibera had a gully that served as a place to throw trash and sewage, because there was no municipal service. The hope was that the rain would wash it away, but of course the rain just spread it around and flooded the shacks at its edge with sewage. Then a community came together with an idea. They would collect their waste, compost it, and sell it as fertilizer. With the profits, they would clean out the gulley and make a channel with gravel held together with wire mesh. There is still poverty, there is still trash, but now when it rains, there is less danger. The water doesn't flood, and if you walk by the gabions, you notice something new. Instead of the muck of a floodplain, there is a soccer field, with bare patches at the goals and very happy kids. Resilient, effective, fun.

Cheonggyecheon, Seoul: Adaptation Transforms a Neighborhood

Seoul, Korea, is an immensely dense city, with endless traffic and endless grey postwar building blocks. But if you go to the Cheonggyecheon, you see a very different city. The Cheonggyecheon is a "day-lighted" river brought back to life to help the flood-prone city handle periods of intense rainfall by beginning the restoration of its watershed infrastructure, much of which had been covered up in the postwar building boom. Sixty years ago, the river had been lined with shanties and used as a sewer.

Then the shanties became concrete-frame buildings and the sewer was paved over with a highway. The new project reverses those moves.

The project surprises you—to come out of a tight side street, and then see the openness, the glittering of the water framed by cream-colored stone promenades, bamboo poking through, kids skipping across the stepping stones. This was not the Seoul I had known before. And those grey buildings? They were quickly being replaced by new works of architecture by Rem Koolhaas and the best of the Korean designers. It's as if the beauty of the river was challenging the buildings and the city to be better. If you sat a moment along the banks, you could see it all come together: the buildings, the nature, and most important, the people. They were lingering, exploring, pointing out a clever fountain detail to their kids, all while going about their business in one of the world's most business-minded cities.

HafenCity, Hamburg: Coordinated Resilience

The new neighborhood of HafenCity in Hamburg, Germany, uses a fascinating combination of adaptation tactics. Located on the site of the city's nineteenth-century docks, no longer viable for twenty-first-century shipping, HafenCity is a new development designed to expand Hamburg's downtown. However, the former dock area is subject to frequent flooding. Tides coupled with North Sea storm surges regularly bring twenty-three-foot rises in the water level. So HafenCity adapted by taking a vertical approach. Buildings are built on top of sunken parking garages so that when the flood is foreseen, cars can drive away. Street levels have to be built up out of the flood zone. Lobby space is built high and dry at the new street elevation. For waterfront buildings (which make up the majority of buildings in the area because the site used to be

dock lands), this means that the building section is asymmetrical. On the water side are two levels of promenade. The lower promenade is meant to flood regularly, and an occasional cafe equipped with flood-proofing devices like a submarine's hatches keeps the promenade lively when open. An upper promenade opens onto the building's lower program level, dry flood-proofed against the rarer flooding to that height with aquarium glass and metal guards against floating debris. On the new street side, the level is high enough to be flood-proof without special devices because it is above the base flood elevation of twenty-eight feet.

Getting these complicated levels to work together required immense coordination, and for the coordination to work required leadership and centralized decision making. The entire neighborhood is being built by a public-private authority led by a man named Jürgen Bruns-Berentelg, who has control over political, financial, and design decisions. Bruns-Berentelg tells the story of trying to determine the base flood elevation so that he could set the proper height of the new streets and begin to build. Realizing that the academic debate on the proper level to avoid flooding might never end, Bruns-Berentelg, as chief executive officer, studied the various scientists' arguments and then made an executive decision that twenty-eight feet above sea level was the proper height. The bulldozers moved in the next day. The buildings are largely complete. The academics are still arguing.

Marina Barrage, Singapore: Turning Risk into Reward

Singapore is at the forefront of adaptation and mitigation efforts at the civic scale. As a city-state, Singapore has no hinterland to draw on, no margin for error in land use decisions. Every square foot of the

city matters, and sometimes multiple goals have to be achieved with the same project because land is the scarcest resource. Every major new project in the city is calibrated to meet all three challenges of growth during climate change: to support a larger, more prosperous population, to reduce the city's carbon emissions, and to adapt the city to survive extreme weather.

Not only are there more people living in Singapore every year, but they expect to live better as well. The city monitors quality-of-life indices and targets improvements in housing, health, education, and nutrition. It also has begun to monitor and improve the quality of public space as an explicit quality-of-life goal for the city. Singapore takes the governmental details of climate change very seriously, having established a National Climate Change Secretariat in the prime minister's office to coordinate adaptation and mitigation. The city has committed to a mitigation target of a 16 percent reduction in carbon emissions by 2020, and the secretariat is performing risk assessments to quantify specific threats to the low-lying city from sea-level rise, permanent temperature shift, and precipitation variability.

Through the blizzard of statistics it generates, the government of Singapore has determined that the best way to secure the city against climate change is to work with nature and not against it, building nature into the very fabric of the city. It recently named the former parks commissioner to be in charge of the city's urban redevelopment agency, the most powerful arm of government in shaping the city. In tropical Singapore, combining nature and urban development gives a new twist to the term "concrete jungle."

Singapore is betting that its success in managing the city is tied to its success in managing the environment. "Managing" is the key word, rather than "protecting," as is typical with government agencies charged with dealing with the environment. Singapore recognizes that the environment is not something so fragile that it has to be insulated from all human activity. Instead, it has to be respected as a powerful force that can either help or hurt human development. To grow while protecting the city from the risks of the natural environment while also protecting the environment from the excesses of human activity is Singapore's mission.

What is fascinating about Singapore's new approach to sustainability is that it includes an explicit policy of improving public space. There is now a marriage between environmental infrastructure and public space infrastructure. Projects engineered to make the city more sustainable are designed also to make the city more livable.

A recently completed public works project, the Marina Barrage, is an example of this new approach to urban design. It is a vital piece of climate

change infrastructure for the city, but it is experienced by the citizen as a walk in the park.

When you approach the Marina Barrage, the first thing you notice is that you don't notice it. The project does not call attention to itself. Unlike the Hoover Dam, it is not a sculptural object that awes you with its scale. You can barely see it. In fact, when you arrive, you are standing on its roof—a green roof, of course. Schoolchildren are picnicking beside you, taking in a spectacular view over a lake bordered by paths and bowers. The lake is a man-made adaptation—it is part of the larger water supply project—sited so that it reflects the skyline of downtown. It is a view that I can only compare to Central Park, the same surprise of towers reflected in a lake surrounded by green. At sunset when the lake is like glass, lovers stroll among the shadows, hushed in the glow of twilight on the water.

Some of the best views of Singapore now come from the barrage. Take a walk down a narrow bridge path, which seems to hop from one small island to the next. These "islands" are actually pumps, and the main building, which served so well as a picnic place, is the pump house, with a command and control center to operate both these pumps as well as a series of gates on the horizon. From this path you can walk through a courtyard where on weekends there are fairs and food festivals and then up a landscaped ramp to the green roof where you dodge kids and their kites. The Marina Barrage looks and acts like an urban park, while in actuality it is a pulsing network of machinery. A museum inside explains the workings.

When I visited Singapore I asked my urban design colleagues at the

Urban Redevelopment Authority how they transformed a piece of engineering infrastructure to be both beautiful and civic. For critical infrastructure protecting the water supply, I would have expected a structure with barbed wire and blank walls. My colleague laughed and said it indeed started that way. The engineers came to the Urban Redevelopment Authority and said they were starting work on the barrage—typical engineers, a big concrete box at the entry to the Singapore River. They wanted planning approval, a formality given the importance of the project. My colleagues told them to wait a minute and started sketching how the pump house roof could be a gathering space, how the sea gate could be a promenade. The engineers were intrigued by the sketches. If it helped speed up the permit, why not build it that way? The sketches are now on exhibit in the museum, etched into the glass background of the text that explains the workings of the pumps.

Can the adaptation of a city to become more resilient be made profitable?

The barrage has lowered Singapore's climate change risk by lowering the consequences of storm surge and sea-level rise. However, the designers have done something very clever. They have pushed the risk away from loss and toward reward, and with the same piece of infrastructure created a real asset for the city—a new supply of freshwater. Located at the delta of a river, the land side of the sea gates sees a constant influx of freshwater. By coordinated use of the main pumps over time, freshwater on the land side can be retained, while saltwater is ejected on the sea side of the gates. This creates a new freshwater lake and drinking water reservoir for Singapore. The creativity in turning a defensive adaption (protecting the city from the sea) into a new resource for the city (a drinking water reservoir) is a striking example of resource creation.

The creativity does not stop with the utility of the reservoir; the park around its edges is also an important new resource for the city. The reservoir has become a scenic lake, and its edges are planted and landscaped.

The barrage is also a tool of mitigation, helping reach Singapore's CDE reduction target. The green roof reduces the amount of energy needed to heat and cool the facility; solar panels provide energy for the lighting. And because the entire facility was built with recycled construction materials, there was relatively little net emission during its construction. Finally, the premise of the infrastructure to be experienced as a park by pedestrians bolsters walkability, reduces auto dependence for recreation, and adds livability to the dense city.

As urban designers, my colleagues couldn't control the engineers, but they figured out how to influence them. Their sketches showed how the project could become not just a climate change improvement but a civic improvement. The Marina Barrage gives us a preview of what a piece of a sustainable city might look like; it is truly a piece of twenty-first-century urban design. But is Singapore exceptional? Could other cities do it?

That may come down to a question of affordability. The financial challenge of urban design in an era of climate change is how to use urban growth to manage risk. Can the adaptation of a city to become more resilient be made profitable? Profit (reward) is related to risk. If you lower your risk, your reward is more certain, and therefore, more valuable. This is why bond prices move inversely with yield. Is there a similar strategy in urban growth? Could we, through acts of adaptation and mitigation, not just avoid the negative but create the positive? As an example, imagine opening your umbrella as an act of adaptation to a sudden storm. Now imagine pushing the umbrella further upwards into a tulip shape. Now you are not only protected from the rain, but you are collecting fresh water. You have created a resource. You have made a positive out of a negative; you have in effect pushed risk into reward. This is what the Marina Barrage has done for Singapore. The creativity embedded in a strategy of resource generation simultaneous with adaptation or mitigation is a hallmark of the new type of urban design that can make cities sustainable and resilient.

What is the monetary value of lower risk? Can it be captured through financial mechanisms of insurance, or perhaps it would require a market in climate adaptation derivatives? If one party is willing to pay a premium to protect against the chance of flood, and another party knows how to build a project that will reduce the consequences or probability of flood (and thereby reduce the chances of ever having to pay out on that premium), don't we have the makings of a deal? Perhaps urban design will have to consider the design of financial instruments as a pertinent field of invention in a century facing the massive expenditures of adaptation.

Red Hook, Brooklyn: Adapting a Neighborhood

"What do I do?," my neighbor on Van Brunt Street asked me this morning as I got on my bike to go into work. He is a carpenter, and his woodshop, his source of livelihood, is in his basement and was under eight feet of water during Hurricane Sandy. Five months after the flood, he had gotten some insurance money and replaced his machines and thought his life was getting back to normal, until he heard a rumor that the federal government had redrawn the flood maps and he would have to buy mandatory federal flood insurance. His insurance would go from $400 to $10,000 a year. "I can't afford that. If the flood didn't put me out of business, the cost of insurance will." He asked again, "What do I do?"

I do not know the answer. The threat of mandatory and ruinous flood insurance is a symptom, not a solution. It's a government policy designed to punish people and keep them from building in dangerous places. Maybe it will work to dissuade people from building mansions on barrier islands, but it has no place being retroactively applied to people who live in brick houses in communities almost three hundred years old.

I have been working for several weeks on plans to rebuild the ground floor of my house. It's frustrating;

Raising the floor to prepare for the next "100-year" storm in Red Hook, Brooklyn. *(Credit: Jessica Levin)*

the rules keep changing. A couple of months ago, the mayor issued an executive order mandating higher levels for rebuilding. Then the federal government issued a new set of standards—advisory base flood elevations—but now these are rumored to be changing. The new flood height is almost five feet above my ground floor. What do I do?

I know for my house that I just want to design in a way that's resilient. When the next flood comes, I want to be able to evacuate, and when I return, get my house back up and running quickly and on my own. So I have come up with ideas for floor panels that I can attach with cables to new ceiling beams, and when the evacuation order comes, I can crank the floor panels up out of the reach of flood waters, with my computers and desk lamps still sitting on my desk, the whole thing going up six feet in the air. When I come back to my house after floodwaters recede, I can hose down my subfloor, dry the place out, and crank the desk back down to its normal position. Should work, but there's nothing in the building code to permit this.

I go around in circles try-ing to understand the city, state, and federal regulations that should tell me how I can rebuild. They all conflict. The insurance company is trying to get out of paying for my loss. I am in a perpetual state of haggling. I am amazed at the number of people I have to deal with. Officials from multiple agencies, banks, insurance companies, contractors, "rapid repair" crews. All are supposed to rebuild, but each re-mains in its silo. It's not the people that are the problem; it's the institutions and the rules that run them. I have never met kinder, more caring govern-ment employees than the adjustor from the Small Business Administration who came to my house and the young loan officer whose voice came from a continent away in California. The people work, but the system is broken.

Shouldn't we be thinking of how together we can best meet the challenge of the new climate realities…?

My neighbor's livelihood depends on his carpentry shop, so he couldn't wait, and he rebuilt as he was before. The rules allow that, the politics en-courage it, but of course it doesn't solve the problem. As a consequence my neighbor is at the mercy of the insurance company. Meanwhile, I am in limbo. Being in limbo at least has given me time to think. Shouldn't we be thinking beyond the capabilities of individual building owners? My puny resources and those of my neighbors are nothing compared to the force of the next storm. Shouldn't we be thinking of how together we can best meet the challenge of the new climate realities, pool our resources, leverage our opportunities, and design our neighborhood to become resilient? If we can do so while still retaining the neighborhood character that defines Red Hook, we will succeed.

Much of the recovery effort since the flood has been focused on just getting back to where we were. And where we were was unprotected. If, in rebuilding our neighborhood, we have neither decreased the probability nor the consequences of disaster, then the risk to our livelihood remains. In the long run, either we move forward as a community and manage our risk, or we fall back into decay and disinvestment if people feel the government has abandoned our neighborhood to its fate. We have to change.

The resilience of Prospect Shore.

(Credit: Jeffrey Shumaker)

Throughout this book, I have maintained that the purpose of urban design is transformation. Can it make my neighborhood resilient? Although it was for a very different purpose, the products and process of urban design transformed the West Chelsea neighborhood. I want to know if the same products and process can transform Red Hook.

Two years ago, we were building computer models to simulate a hurricane strike on New York, and we wrote a playbook for recovery for our realistic but fictitious neighborhood of Prospect Shore. We imagined the process of recovery as a rapid process of transformation, an urban design process. In our computer scenario, we imagined that the old brick buildings in the neighborhood that survived the storm were hardened with reinforcing steel and integrated into new hurricane-resistant building structures. The new buildings would have ground floors reserved for retail. The geometry of their envelopes would be optimized to withstand wind forces. The new streets and buildings in Prospect Shore would drain into a restored waterway where native plants would bioremediate any toxins before they reached the harbor. Industry would be rebuilt at the waterfront, but in the future it would be integrated with a public esplanade and protected from storm surge by an earthen levee doubling as a park. Wetlands would take root offshore and a barrier island in the harbor would become an oyster habitat. We imagined in our computer scenario that we succeeded. Residents and new neighbors returned to find Prospect Shore physically better prepared for storms, socially better integrated into the surrounding city, and therefore more sustainable and resilient than before.

The realities of transforming Red Hook are sobering when compared with the computer simulations of Prospect Shore. Everything having to do with recovery is at least three times more complicated. Instead of one level of government trying to take the lead, there are three, and the city, state, and federal agencies are already putting out competing plans. Instead of one time frame to accomplish the goals of redevelopment, there are three: an emergency recovery time frame we are in now, an interim housing and coastal protection time frame that could last years, and a permanent time frame to build a successful shield against climate change that will need to endure well into the century. Finally, any plans we make to reduce the consequences of flooding require sharing risk across three different scales of adaptation: building-scale projects, neighborhood-scale projects, and regional-scale projects.

There is confusion. The federal government is rushing to put out new flood maps. While the mapped flood elevations change, the city is trying to process building permits based on shifting data. Meanwhile, private insurance companies are redlining any neighborhood within three thousand feet of water. And with no insurance, no mortgage, the only option is federal insurance, but if your building doesn't meet federal standards, the cost of that insurance is too much for most people to afford. New building regulations may outlaw residential income units on the ground floor. Property values might plummet. Everyone is nervous. We are approaching a crisis of confidence: we perceive the problem to be that we have no consensus to solve the problem.

. . . we perceive the problem to be that we have no consensus to solve the problem.

But that is an illusion. Fear should not be confused with confusion. We have the tools, the products, and process to succeed. West Chelsea can serve as a model. We have the resources: more than $54 billion are earmarked for projects in our region alone. If we design it right, we can link a public project through changes in zoning and transportation into private investment that will achieve our resilience goals and improve the quality of our public space. Whether we can grow into resilience and yet preserve the character of our neighborhood is the question.

The High Line Project and the Special West Chelsea District are successful examples of the products and process of urban design applied to the transformation of a neighborhood, and they can be applied to Red Hook.

Outdated Federal Emergency Management Agency flood map of Red Hook, Brooklyn.

In the Red Hook timeline we will see the nested, iterative process of urban design where politics, finance, and design intersect. We will see how the same process of stating the problem, designing the answer, and then implementing the solution plays out almost simultaneously at every scale and across every product of urban design. Whether it will be a rule (e.g., a policy change to support the strengthening of our coastline or the zoning text establishing the rules for new resilient building), a plan (e.g., an economic study to show how risk and reward can be shared between public improvements and private owners or the final design showing where each line of defense against storm surge will be placed), or a product (e.g., the construction of a greenway, park, or seawall or the building of the first resilient building that both protects from flood and promotes the walkability of the neighborhood), each product of urban design has a role in the process of making Red Hook resilient.

In the Red Hook scenario, we will see which products of urban design play which role when. We will discover what vision can redefine the "client" from the existing families of sparsely populated Red Hook to a million people across the region who come to view our future success as a model for their own community's rebirth. We will see how government agencies can enlarge the notion of "site" from our individual row houses struggling to flood-proof by ourselves into a neighborhood and even regional system of shared public spaces and resiliency projects, each designed to counter a specific threat of climate change. We will see how tools of zoning or finance (e.g., insurance, mortgage, and taxation) could be used positively, not punitively, to support change so that the "program" escalates from millions in public improvements to billions in private investment. For Red Hook to become resilient before the next storm comes, each product of urban design will have to be a discreet, actionable instrument to shift the ground, to change the rules of the game, to make transformation happen.

The Three Judges of Urban Design

If we succeed, how would the three great urban designers of New York's history judge our accomplishments? I call them my three bosses; as an urban designer, I haven't succeeded unless they are satisfied. So I ask myself, what would Moses, Jacobs, and Olmsted think of a transformation of Red Hook to be resilient and sustainable?

I think Robert Moses would appreciate a financing mechanism that could pay for the massive costs of adaptation by tapping into the value created by lowering risk to a city. He would be impressed that transformation could happen simultaneously at the scale of individual buildings, coastal parks, and regional infrastructure. He was a master builder of all three.

I think Jane Jacobs would be impressed if we could maintain the character of our streets while making ground floor uses resilient to flood. Our curious mix of people and buildings, old timers and artist families, brick warehouses, piers, and housing projects will either slowly be abandoned or it will be transformed into something vital and durable, livable and sustainable primarily because of how it is perceived at the street level, by the pedestrian. Perhaps the tall, old brick warehouses that have survived the last 150 years here give a clue to a possible building form for future resilience. If they had reinforced concrete frames behind their bricks, and if their rusty arched metal shutters could be replaced with stouter versions that would dry flood-proof the ground floor when closed, then—with shutters

HURRICANE SANDY
RED HOOK'S STORM SURGE
OCTOBER 29, 2012 • 6:00 PM TO 12:00 AM

0.00   Land elevation (in feet)

Street

Flooded street
(entire or partial)

Storm surge flow

------- TIMELINE -------

1   6:00: Valentino Park floods to the end of Coffey Street.

2   6:40: Storm surge from the Upper Bay reaches Van Dyke and Van Brunt streets.

3   7:00-7:30: Seawater from Buttermilk Channel swamps Van Brunt Street between Commerce and Pioneer; then flooding continues along Van Brunt to Wolcott.

4   7:39: Dry Dock loses power.

5   7:40: The surge driven north on Columbia Street splits in two. One section spills over the wall at the back of the ball fields, then runs across Red Hook Recreation Area toward Lorraine Street. The other courses toward Red Hook Community Farm.

6   9:22: Floodwaters recede from 125 Coffey Street; it takes until midnight before water levels drop significantly at 259 Van Brunt Street.

7   9:40: Roughly 50 minutes after high tide, the surge stops at 64 West 9th Street, a Zone B location.

8   According to Port Authority Police, the surge stops at Bowne and Hamilton, Seabring and Columbia, and the steps of Chase Bank. Floodwaters do not enter the Brooklyn-Battery Tunnel from the Brooklyn side.

9   The surge extends for one mile along Columbia Street, from its southern elbow, near IKEA, to the front door of Defonte's Sandwich Shop at Luquer Street.

10   Measured from street level to high-water mark, Fairway Market had nearly a six-foot river flow along its Van Brunt Street side.

13.88 ft   Storm surge peak
(9:24 at the Battery in Lower Manhattan)

75 mph   Maximum sustained winds

SOURCES: GOOGLE MAPS; JIM MCMAHON; NOAA; OPEN STREET MAP; ELEVATION CHART: ELEVATION FOR REAL; ELEVATION PRO: USGS. MAGARET PHILLIPS, HYDROLOGICAL TECHNICIAN. SOME ELEVATIONS ROUNDED.

FLOOD SOURCES: SALAH ALAMRI; SUNNY BALZANO; ABRAHAM BARAKAT; TRICIANNI BOTTA; LISA BRODY; SETH BRODY; BROOKLYN CRAB; MICHAEL BUSCEMI; MONICA BYRNE; COLUMBIA STREET CAR SERVICE; FAMILY SUPERMARKET; FDNY ENGINE 202/LADDER 101; FDNY ENGINE 279/LADDER 131; FINE FARE SUPERMARKET; FLUNG WAH TRANSPORT; RICHARD GILLIARD; GLORY TRADING CORP; CARY GOLDSTEIN; GINA GUSBY; SHARON GUSBY; JOFAZ TRANSPORTATION; TONE JOHANSEN; FRANCIS KERRIGAN; MARIJKA KOSTIW; APOLLINA KYLE; MARY DUDINE KYLE; RON KYLE; HUNG VAN LA; IAN MARVY; JOHN MCGETTRICK (CO-CHAIRMAN OF THE RED HOOK CIVIC ASSOCIATION); HELEN MCMAHON; JIM MCMAHON; CAROLINE MOORE; KEVIN MOORE; KEVIN MULKEREN; NEW WAY DELI & GROCERY; 990 DREAMS; BARRY O'MEARA; GUILLO ONNA (2012 GROUNDSKEEPER OF THE YEAR, RED HOOK RECREATION AREA); BARBARA PEAKS; PASCAL PERICH; SCOTT PFAFFMAN; RAINGER PINNEY; FRAN PISANO; PORT AUTHORITY OF NEW YORK & NEW JERSEY; BROOKLYN-BATTERY TUNNEL; WILLIAM ROBERTSON; MATT ROSS; CAROLINA SALGUERG (PORTSIDE NEW YORK); BEN SCHNEIDER; DAVID SHARPS (WATERFRONT MUSEUM); STATEWIDE OIL & HEATING; MARC TAUSS; TONY TAVARES SR; U.S. FRIED CHICKEN; U.S. POSTAL SERVICE; GINO VITALE (RED HOOK DEVELOPER); YVONNE WALKER; KARIN WEINER; ANYA YURCHYSHYN; AND A NOD TO KATHY WILMORE.

MAP: JIM MCMAHON, CARTOGRAPHER (RED HOOK RESIDENT: FIVE YEARS ON WEST 9TH STREET, ZONE B; THREE YEARS ON COFFEY STREET, ZONE A) AND ONE OF SEVERAL EYEWITNESSES TO THE STORM SURGE) ©2012.

DEDICATED TO ALL CURRENT AND FUTURE RESIDENTS OF RED HOOK.

CO-PUBLISHED BY JIM MCMAHON, HOME/MADE, AND KENTLER INTERNATIONAL DRAWING SPACE.

Map of the storm-surge damage from Sandy made by a resident of Red Hook, Brooklyn. *(Credit: Map by Jim McMahon)* open—we could maintain much of the street activity that makes the neighborhood a delight on a summer's day, when strollers peer into artists' workshops and storehouses on the quayside. Jane would judge us on how we amplify the density of our pedestrian experience throughout the neighborhood, and yet maintain the diversity of the smaller buildings also dating back to the nineteenth century, like my own old row house. If a clever way to temporarily raise the floor can make my ground floor both active and safe, she would approve. She would not approve if I took the easy way out and converted my Victorian storefront into a parking garage.

Finally, Frederick Law Olmsted would want to see if we can harness natural systems for coastal protection while giving our city a new public park. Some people have talked of oyster beds and wetlands, perhaps Dutch-style polders offshore with gates to let in water and boats, or seawalls with greenways built along their crests. All would have to be public, all would have to lower the risk from storm to the buildings and families inland. Long term, I think Olmsted would be pleased if this natural infrastructure were a catalyst as well, an emerald necklace for the coastline of twenty-first-century New York.

At the moment, though, we have only questions, not accomplishments. The judges are my family and my neighbors. They ask me daily how can our low-lying coastal neighborhood become sustainable as a place to live, raise children, and maintain a business? My neighbors make a great variety of products for their livelihood, from marine tools to art and ideas. One makes maps; he's made the most accurate map yet of the flood damage relying on the accounts of his neighbors rather than the images of satellites.

We just want to be free from the fear that every year may bring a storm that would destroy everything we have made, making a lifetime of investment little more secure than building an afternoon's sand castle. We see it as a local problem for Red Hook, but if we can come up with a solution that works here, it could go global. Much of the world's population lives in low-lying coastal cities where neighborhoods like mine are less than a few meters above sea level.

My neighbors and I are only slowly becoming aware of the enormity of our challenge, the difficulty of making politics, finance, and design align long enough in New York City to change our neighborhood and make it resilient, while preserving the character of our community and the quality of our public space. In that realization, my neighbors are discovering something new: that they, too, are becoming urban designers.

Prague's waterfront paving includes anchors for deployable flood walls that can protect the city's historic center from twenty-first-century storm events. (Credit: Alexandros Washburn)

Flood wall as park; Copenhagen's historic defense walls offer a precedent.
(Credit: Alexandros Washburn)

A view of Sydney Harbor.

(Credit: Alexandros Washburn)

Sandy floodwaters outside of
the author's home.
(Credit: Alexandros Washburn)

The highway in downtown Seoul, South Korea, was torn down to allow for the restoration of the Cheonggyecheon River, which has revitalized the area. (Credit: Photo by Julia K. Bass, 2012)

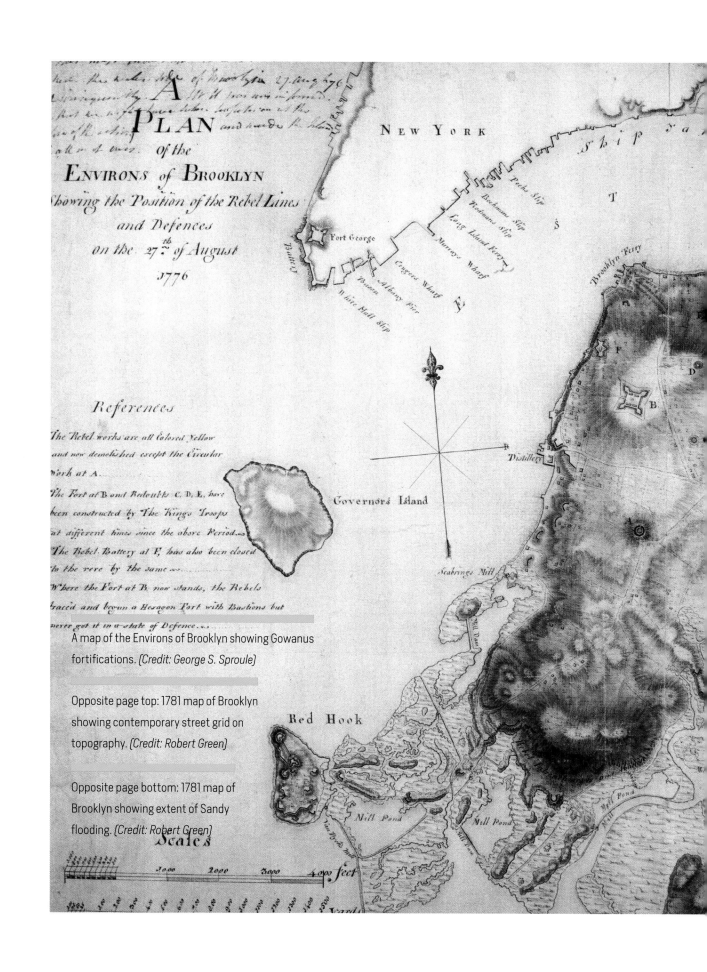

A map of the Environs of Brooklyn showing Gowanus fortifications. *(Credit: George S. Sproule)*

Opposite page top: 1781 map of Brooklyn showing contemporary street grid on topography. *(Credit: Robert Green)*

Opposite page bottom: 1781 map of Brooklyn showing extent of Sandy flooding. *(Credit: Robert Green)*

Top: Views of Hong Kong.

(Credit: Alexandros Washburn)

Bottom: Red Hook Community Farm.

(Credit: Alexandros Washburn)

Favela child, Brazil.

(Credit: Davis Thompson–Moss)

ivic virtue is the cultivation of habits important for the success of the community. Cities are shaped by urban design to reflect what each society considers to be its civic virtues. At a time when the resilience of urban growth during climate change is our foremost challenge, we need to adapt, mitigate, and generate renewable resources in our cities. In such a time, the simple human traits of prudence, thrift, and creativity could be elevated to the role of civic virtues. Inherent in the concept of civic virtue is selflessness. The one who pays is not the one who is rewarded. Cities take a long time to build, so one generation must act for the benefit of the next. Civic virtue must be durable.

In ancient times, civilizations learned to express civic virtue through architecture. Will we, like the ancient Greeks before us, design buildings that embody our idea of sustainable civic virtue? Or instead of architecture, will the design language that will both express and activate these virtues become urban design?

The Greeks may not have invented civic virtue, but they certainly branded the idea with architecture. Think Corinthian column, and you can not help but think of grand civic buildings of the past. The story goes that the inventor of the Corinthian column capital was inspired by nature, by the curl of the acanthus leaf. Corinthian became the standard for public buildings of the first rank, such as the Pantheon in Rome. It was so costly to carve that its use on a building became proof of the civic virtue of its builder. When someone wished to be seen as doing something good for a city, he built a building with classical architecture.

That classical architecture remained synonymous with civic virtue for more than two thousand years is testament to its enduring power and universal appeal. As late as the beginning of the twentieth century, when the federal government wanted to show New York just how much it valued the city, it built a monumental post office to express its civic virtue. The Farley Building, built in 1913, boasts the longest giant-order Corinthian colonnade in the world.

As much as we may admire the classical architecture of the Farley Building, we would not choose to recreate its colonnade today if we wished to express civic virtue. The brand has been diluted. Putting a Corinthian column on your building has lost its meaning. The Corinthian column no longer signifies virtue, civic or otherwise. There has been a paradigm shift away from architecture. What signifies virtue these days is a concern for nature. If you care about your city today, you do not just build a building; you build a green building. Nature is the new civic virtue.

This is a vision of a new type of city for the twenty-first century: at once more urbane and more natural. It is a marriage of building and landscape that is challenging every notion we have ever had about design. In a grove of trees in Battery Park City, where you can feel lost in a forest while being a few blocks from Wall Street, you feel that nature and the city are one.

The paradigm of civic virtue has shifted to nature, and we must change our direction to follow. Indeed, to lead. Just as two millennia ago, a sculptor transformed the biomass of the acanthus plant into a template for architecture, today we must transform the rigidities of architecture into the natural adaptations of cities. The stone column crumbles and is replaced with the growing stalk. Networks of green signify community in ways that the architecture of the past no longer can. Urban design centers around the nature of new public spaces, often wrestled from the automobile, furnished for the pedestrian and crafted in consultation with the community they serve. Nature is invited into these spaces, whether to cool them with foliage, to channel their storm water, or simply to use the sun to best advantage. The result is that even the densest cities are filing with oases, and nature at all scales is being discovered as the urban design secret to transmute the quantity of urban density into the quality of civic life.

THE ART OF URBAN DESIGN

When our competence in the techniques and strategies of urban design matures, when we get good enough at building a piece of the public realm that we can make it beautiful even as we make it practical, that is the moment urban design can become art.

The leap from practical to beautiful is the leap from archaic to classical. The archaic period is when an art form works out its techniques and sets its aspirations, like the ancient Greek sculptors who first carved the stiff but noble statues of the seventh century B.C. The leap to classical sculpture came two hundred years later, under Pericles, and it marked the point when the art of ancient Greece became a universal standard and defined a culture.

The leap from archaic to classic is what makes or breaks an art, the moment when truth becomes beauty and beauty, truth. I see that moment ahead for the nature of urban design, although given the slow gestation of city building, the leap may not come in the next generation or even the next. Urban design is not there yet as an art; we are struggling in an archaic phase where we are asking the right questions, setting our aspirations, making our first noble attempts at transformation of cities toward both beauty and resilience. But we don't even have our system of measures set; we have far to go to sharpen our chisels and strike with absolute precision. We are in an era of approximation.

The ancient Greeks gave the world a system of ethics that they made visible as civic virtue in their architecture. Now we ask what is our society's relation to nature? This question is forced upon us because of climate change. Cities affect climate, and climate affects cities. If climate change threatens

our cities, of necessity we will answer the question through the design of our cities. This is not a "once in a lifetime" question. It is a once in a civilization question.

CITY FUTURES

Our technocratic culture tends to imagine a city of tomorrow as a place that springs out of nowhere. Masdar is a $24 billion city now being built in the desert patch between Abu Dhabi and its airport in the United Arab Emirates. It is meant to be a no-carbon city, a vast experiment in sustainability financed by a government with one of the world's largest concentrations of fossil fuels.

But is Masdar the city of the future, or is it something more akin to Burnham's White City at the 1893 World's Fair in Chicago? An inspiration, a model, perhaps, but not a living city. There are plenty of other contenders for the "city of the future" title, ranging from Tianjin outside of Beijing to Sam-dong outside of Seoul. They all involve a lot of money, a lot of consultants, and a lot of land. These new urban areas, such as Masdar, are planned entirely top-down. They look to technology as the answer to an unsustainable urban present, and their empty sites give them a clean slate where they might sidestep the mistakes of the past.

But even when fully populated, these entirely new cities will account for only a tiny fraction of the world's urban growth. Most of the world's growth will occur in the thousands of already established cities, places where you can't walk away from the past, where transformation is difficult, where inadequacy is everywhere.

The existing urban landscape with all of its problems retains one insurmountable advantage over these blueprint cities: citizens who are already there. They desire change. They want their lives to be better. They want their cities to be more livable: safer, more equitable, with more opportunity to achieve their potential and secure the promise of their children. They don't necessarily know or care about sustainability. They just want better lives. That's why they came to the city in the first place. And if the city itself, with rotten sewers and dangerous streets, stands in their way, then the city itself must change.

Desire leads to change. Change leads to opportunity. A city without desire is a stagnant city, and there will be no change for better or worse. But in a city where there is a desire for livability there is an opportunity for sustainability. Make a city livable, and in the process it can become sustainable. Recognize that the desire to improve the quality of civic life opens the door to change. If we as citizens and urban designers can shape that change to make our cities sustainable, we will have performed a great service. Everyone, from our families to our planet, will benefit. I just want to emphasize how the process begins with a bottom-up desire to make life better, and it continues with a top-down technical understanding of how to achieve it. But we can't just build a Masdar in the desert and imagine the problem solved.

Though there is a great desire for change among the people who live in cities, they have few tools to affect that change. If those people can learn the basics of urban design and city building and so find a place where they can participate in the systems that change their cities, they will change them for the better. When it comes to technology to make the future city, I would rather have social media and smartphones in a favela than solar cells in Masdar. When people are connected with their neighbors and their leaders and feel that their voice is heard and their city is malleable to their intentions (at whatever scale, from regional infrastructure to neighborhood planting), resignation to the status quo rapidly becomes resolve for civic improvement. If you want to see the future of cities, don't go to Masdar. Go to a favela in São Paulo, and look into the eyes of a child standing on a trash pile. That is where the desire for change will come from. And the trash pile is where the city of tomorrow will be built.

As a designer, I can speculate on what the future city will look like. I hope each city will be livable, sustainable, and different from every other. I hope each neighborhood will grow locally with local designers to become more resilient while remaining unique and celebrating its character. Let cities be diverse.

I hope this book can become a framework for meeting ecological goals globally while expressing civic intent through design locally in each city. There is no single design answer, but there are shared human values and shared human proportions that help us sort through our options. I believe those values center on prudence, thrift, and creativity, but the social and aesthetic culture of each city will interpret them differently. Closest to home, these values are really no more than a reminder to love your neighborhood as you love your family, to defend it and change it for the better for each succeeding generation.

Manhattanhendge: the setting sun aligns with the street grid of the city twice per year.
(Credit: Alexandros Washburn)

If we hold and act on these values, they will rise to the level of civic virtues. I believe there is an innate desire in humans to change things for the better, and that for so many of the world's citizens, there is a stifling inability to change their surroundings. Whether it's the vacuity of too much material riches or the constraints of poverty that is to blame, the effect is the same: an inability to change things, a frustrated desire for true malleability in our cities. I'd like to think that the transformative power of urban design can crack open the status quo, and in so doing give opportunity for the birth of civic virtue in places that have none. And in those places where civic virtue flourished, urban design will translate those virtues into the built and natural forms around us. We shape our cities, and our cities shape us.

Introduction

[1] Richard Dobbs, Sven Smit, Jaana Remes, James Manyika, Charles Rox-
    burgh, and Alejandra Restrepo, "Urban World: Mapping the Economic
    Power of Cities," McKinsey Global Institute, March 2011. http://www
    .mckinsey.com/insights/urbanization/urban_world.

[2] Jinjun Xue and Wenshu Gao, "How Large is the Urban-Rural Income Gap
    in China?," http://faculty.washington.edu/karyiu/confer
    /sea12/papers/SC12-110%20Xue_Guo.pdf.

[3] http://uil.unesco.org/fileadmin/keydocuments/Literacy/LIFE/Midterm
    Package/8_statistical_data_on_Literacy/4UIS_LIFE_urban
    _rural_graph_2011.pdf.

[4] Nate Berg, "U.S. Urban Population Is Up . . . But What Does 'Urban' Really
    Mean?," Atlantic Cities, March 26, 2012. http://www
    .theatlanticcities.com/neighborhoods/2012/03/us-urban
    -population-what-does-urban-really-mean/1589/.

[5] U.S. Department of Transportation, Federal Highway Administration,
    Dwight D. Eisenhower National System of Interstate and Defense
    Highways, http://www.fhwa.dot.gov/programadmin/interstate
    .cfm.

Chapter 1: Why Should We Care about Cities?

[1] New York City Panel on Climate Change, "Climate Risk Information," Feb-
    ruary 17, 2009. http://www.nyc.gov/html/om/pdf/2009/NPCC
    _CRI.pdf.

[2] What If New York City, Urban Post-Disaster Housing Prototype Program,
    http://www.nyc.gov/html/whatifnyc/html/home/home
    .shtml.

[3] Brooklyn Grange, http://www.brooklyngrangefarm.com/.

[4] Eric Sanderson, *Mannahatta: A Natural History of New York City* (New York: Abrams, 2009).

[5] Federal Writers' Project, *The WPA Guide to New York City: The Federal Writers' Project Guide to 1930s New York* (New York: New Press, 1995).

Chapter 2: The Process of Urban Design

[1] Carol Burns and Andrea Kahn, "Introduction," in *Site Matters,* Burns and Kahn, ed. (London: Routledge, 2005), xii. I use "influence" to refer to the largest scale because influence is diffuse and difficult to measure. I use "effect" to refer to the intermediate scale because an effect should be measurable and mappable to its cause.

[2] The Vertical Farm, http://www.verticalfarm.com/.

[3] Nikos Salingaros, *Principles of Urban Structure* (Amsterdam: Techne Press, 2005), p. 227.

Chapter 3: The Products of Urban Design

[1] Chris Rado and Uttam Berra, "Reinventing 1961 New York City Zoning," ESRI User Conference Proceedings, 2012. http://proceedings.esri.com /library/userconf/proc12/papers/65_132.pdf.

[2] E. Larson, *The Devil in the White City* (Random House, 2004). http://www. randomhouse.com/crown/devilinthewhitecity/burnham.html.

[3] Charles Moore, *The Life and Times of Charles Follen McKim* (Houghton Mifflin Co., 1929).

[4] Simon Romero, "Medellín's Nonconformist Mayor Turns Blight to Beauty," *New York Times,* July 15, 2007. http://www .nytimes.com/2007/07/15/world/americas/15medellin .html?pagewanted=all&_r=0.

[5] Kayden, Jerold S. and the NYC Department of City Planning and the Municipal Art Society. *Privately Owned Public Space: The New York City Experience.* New York: John Wiley, 2000. http://www.apops.mas.org

Chapter 4: The Process and Products of the High Line

[1] Albert Amateau, "High Line Rolls Up Numbers; Visitors Top 2 Million Mark," *The Villager,* April 7–13, 2010, Vol. 79, No. 44. http://www .thevillager.com/villager_362/highline.html.

2 High Line Blog, "2012 at the High Line in Photos," Dec. 27, 2012. http://www.thehighline.org/blog/2012/12/27/2012-at-the-high-line-in-photos.

3 "Construction Begins on Architect Jean Nouvel's 'Vision Machine' along Manhattan's West Side," April 8, 2007. http://wirednewyork.com/forum/showthread.php?t=13300.

4 David Sokol, "HL23: High Line Hosts a First for Neil Denari," *Architectural Record,* April 2008. http://archrecord.construction.com/news/OnTheBoards/0804hl23.asp.

5 "100 11th Avenue," *Architectural Record,* http://archrecord.construction.com/projects/building_types_study/multi-family-housing/2011/100-11th-avenue.asp.

6 Alexander Walter, "HL23 to open on June 1," *Archinect,* March 9, 2011. http://archinect.com/news/article/105046/hl23-to-open-on-june-1.

Chapter 5: Urban Design for Greater Resilience

1 IPCC, Core Writing Team, R. K. Pachauri and A. Reisinger, eds., "Climate Change 2007: Synthesis Report. Contribution of Working Groups I, II and III to the Fourth Assessment Report of the Intergovernmental Panel on Climate Change" (Geneva, Switzerland: IPCC).

2 Christopher Leinberger, *The Option of Urbanism* (Washington, D.C.: Island Press, 2007).

3 Shlomo Angel, with Jason Parent, Daniel L. Civco, and Alejandro M. Blei, "Making Room for a Planet of Cities" (Cambridge, Mass.: Lincoln Institute of Land Policy, 2011). http://community-wealth.org/_pdfs/articles-publications/outside-us/report-angel-et-al.pdf.

4 Projjal Dutta, Metropolitan Transit Authority, State of New York, Taking the Subway to Copenhagen—How Transit Is Essential to Global GHG Reduction, http://www.railvolution.org/rv2009_pdfs/20091030_2pm_ToGreenOrNot_Dutta.pdf.

5 Women Are Heroes, Brazil. http://www.jr-art.net/projects/women-are-heroes-brazil.

6 Eric Klinenberg, *Heat Wave: A Social Autopsy of Disaster in Chicago* (Chicago: University of Chicago Press, 2002).

INDEX

Brooklyn Bridge Park, 127
Brooklyn Grange, 29, 177, 189
Brooklyn Heights, 12, 38
Brooklyn-Battery Tunnel, 12
Brown, Denise Scott, 113
brownfields, 127
Bruns-Berentelg, Jürgen, 192
Budapest, 43f
building codes, 52, 102–103, 199
building design
    green, 171, 173–174, 176–177
    mitigation through, 173–177
    building information systems,
    22
bulk regulations, 107, 108, 142
    algorithmic, 110
    High Line, 145, 148–149
    resource generation and, 178
    solar zoning and, 114
Burden, Amanda, 84, 140, 141, 148
Burnham, Daniel, 117, 118
bus rapid transit, 84f, 166, 169
Byzantium, 185

cameras, 64, 66
Campidoglio, 70
Canada, Geoffrey, 76–78
carbon capture, 179–180
carbon counts, 188
carbon dioxide equivalent (CDE),
    162, 176
    density and, 163
    pedestrian mobility and, 167
    Singapore targets for, 196
carbon emissions, 28f, 29
    resiliency and, 40–41
    walkability and, 89
carbon footprint, 29, 175

CDE. *See* carbon dioxide
    equivalent
census tracts, 22
Central Park, 37, 41, 71, 127, 195
Champs Élysée, 70
charrette, 74f–75f, 75
charter schools, 78
Cheonggyecheon, Seoul, Korea,
    191–192, 211f
Chicago Loop, 44f–45f
China
    cities in, 6, 18
    green building labeling in, 173
Chrysler Building, 72, 106, 107f, 171
cities
    adaptation tactics, 181
    Aristotle on, 15
    attraction of, 16
    baroque, 98
    bounding, 21–24
    comparing, 21
    defining, 18–19
    density of, 21
    fractal, 98–99
    futures of, 222–224
    growth patterns of, 51
    importance of, 5
    learning about, 11
    migration to, 16
    as part of nature, 24–25
    polycentric, 168
    resilience of, 8
    size of, 19
    statistical units of, 18
    suburbs as, 6
    vulnerability of, 7–8
City: Rediscovering the Center
    (Whyte), 125

civic virtue, 217–219, 224
classical period, 219
Clean Air Act, 25
Clean Water Act, 25
client, 52, 54, 55f
    identifying, 56–57
    site and, 59–60
    stakeholders as, 75, 77
climate adaptation derivatives,
    197
climate change
    cities affected by, 25–26
    cities effect on, 27–29
    coastal city vulnerability to, 17
    mitigation strategies, 9
    risk profiles and, 85, 188, 196
    Singapore and, 193–194, 196
    social resilience to, 184
    testing and, 82
    urban design process and, 87
    walkability and, 89
cloud-sourcing, 190
coastal cities, 30, 205
    climate change vulnerability
    of, 17
cogeneration, 175
COHAB, 184
collegiality, 74–75, 80
community groups, 57
Coney Island
    redevelopment planning, 81
    rezoning plans, 68f–69f
Constantinople, 7, 182, 185
Copenhagen, 207f
Corinthian column, 218
Corner, James, 126
Cracolandia, 183
Crédit Foncier, 53

ABOUT THE AUTHOR

As Chief Urban Designer of New York's Department of City Planning, Alexandros Washburn has been at the forefront of Mayor Michael Bloomberg's epic remaking of the city. World traveler, global professor, and bicycle commuter, he takes his sketchbook with him to cities around the world looking for best practices to bring home to New York City.

The challenge of resilience is something he is addressing both professionally and personally—his own house in Red Hook, Brooklyn was flooded by Hurricane Sandy. To meet this challenge he relies on his experience in a career made up of equal parts politics, finance and design: government staffer for the late Senator Moynihan; community developer and urban farmer in Durham, North Carolina; and design principal with national awards in urban design, architecture and landscape architecture, including the prestigious Public Architect Award from the New York chapter of the American Institute of Architects.

His goal is to meet the challenges of the day while improving the quality of civic life, and by writing this book, widen the circle of those who can learn to change cities for the better.

(Credit: Colin Gardner)